Being Palestinian Makes Me Smile

Amer Zahr

Published in the United States
by SIMSIM PUBLISHING, LLC

ISBN 978-0-9914679-2-1

www.amerzahr.com
www.civilarab.com

Cover design by Amer Zahr

For George, Anan,
Imad, Salma, & Laila

Acknowledgments

I have many people to thank for the construction of this work. They are the stubbornly Palestinian role models I have had throughout my life. They are strong, enduring, tenacious, persevering, and resolute. They have taught me how to be Palestinian.

This list is definitely incomplete.

Thanks to George and Anan.

Thanks to Elias, Salma, Muhammad, and Laila.

Thanks to Janette, Khowla, Najwa, and Omaima.

Thanks to Rashad, Jamaal, Jawaad, Emran, Jihan, Nisreen, Amani, Samar, Reem, Elias, Nur, and Fadi.

Thanks to Shawqi and Nadira.

Thanks to Bassam and Alice. Thanks to Tawfiq and Malak. Thanks to Ali and Shams. Thanks to Haytham and Andaleeb. Thanks to George and Mary. Thanks to Abed and Nisreen.

Thanks to Hanna, Suzan, Maher, Alma, Kamal, Anan, Mohammad, Riyad, Nael, Ruba, and Samer.

Also, thanks to my good friend Fay for her invaluable help and suggestions in preparing the passages herein.

Introduction

This book has been over 4 years in the making. The passages here are taken from my blog, "The Civil Arab" (www.civilarab.com). I have included the original dates of posting. At times, the pieces have been slightly modified for this work. In other words, if, in hindsight, I found a particular paragraph or sentence to be not as convincing, humorous, or moving as I would have liked, I modified it for your benefit. You're welcome!

What you are about to read is a mixture of political analysis, autobiography, and reflection. And I throw in jokes whenever I think they are appropriate. As it turns out, I often think they are appropriate. As a Palestinian, it can be very easy to become consumed by depression and despair. But I have always noticed that laughter and crying are not as different as they might seem. We have all seen people laugh so hard that they begin to cry. But have you ever seen people cry so hard that they begin to laugh? I have. See, not that different.

Also, I do not hate Jews. This is a standard disclaimer for any Palestinian who writes or comments on Palestinian or Israeli-related issues. Of course, those who will see my comments criticizing Israel as anti-Semitic probably won't be comforted by that qualification, but I thought I would give it nonetheless.

Finally, I am not some recluse or hermit. I am a comedian and I love audiences. I tell jokes in the hopes of being heard, and I write in the hopes of being read. So, thank you.

Enjoy.

(Updated November 2014)

Contents

An open letter to Jon Stewart

November 19, 2009

Jon, I've been watching you.

First, thank you for airing the interview you conducted with Mustafa Barghouti and Anna Baltzer. I'm sure your staff received thousands of letters from Arab-Americans thanking you for airing that piece. I'm also sure you received many letters from viewers chastising you for "allowing" such voices on the air. You might wonder why we were so jubilant that something like that got on TV. Well, it's because nothing like that ever gets on TV. So, thanks!

And like I said, I've been watching you. Aside from being a comedic influence on me (Yes, I watched "You Wrote It, You Watch It"), I rarely miss an episode of the *The Daily Show*. I always notice the remarks you make about our wars in Iraq and Afghanistan, and I pay special attention to anything you ever say about the Palestinian-Israeli conflict. You are always levelheaded, fair, and funny. As a Palestinian-American, frankly, I get excited listening to what you have to say. Your words have a greater weight because you are a recognizable American voice, but more importantly, because you are a recognizable Jewish-American voice. As you know, whenever a Jew or Palestinian speaks on the Palestinian-Israeli conflict, it has a different sort of gravity.

There's something important to understand about us Palestinians in America. We are constantly disappointed, constantly feeling slighted, constantly getting misrepresented. Frankly, whenever we hear a Palestinian voice is going to be on TV, we immediately assume it will be attacked, trapped, or discredited. Your willingness to provide an open and honest forum for Barghouti and Baltzer to speak was not only a breath of fresh air, but also a courageous act, whether you meant it to be or not.

So Jon, I've been watching you... and all I have to say is: Come out of the closet, already! Come over to our side! It will feel better, I promise. I see it in you. You have a nagging attraction to truth and justice. You're perfect for us! You have what many people find an annoying high level of humanity and conscience. C'mon, you know you really want to openly hold Israel responsible for occupation, and separate the legit-

3

imate and just cause of the Palestinian people from their incompetent and corrupt leadership. My commitment comes not from the fact that I am Palestinian, but rather from the strong belief that I'm on the right side. It lets me sleep better at night. You will too!

As you well know, in a sort of wicked irony, the Palestinian experience has come to mimic the Jewish experience. Palestinians and Jews now share more than just a political conflict that has stretched for much of the past century; they also share a history of refuge, discrimination, diaspora and powerlessness. The Palestinian has inherited the Jewish political soul, made to feel like a foreigner in his own land, battered by his enemy, abandoned by his protectors, and left to fend for himself against incredible odds.

Jon, as you also know, the problem in most analyses of the Israeli-Palestinian conflict is that they rest on faulty assumptions. The first is an assumption of parity, and Israel knowingly forwards this misconception. What we are talking about when referring to the relationship between Palestinians and Israelis is not the relationship of one nation with another, but rather of a military occupying power with a civilian occupied populace.

Also, Jon, most speak as if the Palestinians and Israelis have equal control. In other words, most discourses revolve around the incorrect supposition that the Israelis control Israel and that the Palestinians control Gaza and the West Bank, while in fact Israel exercises complete military control in most of the West Bank and Gaza and complete discretion in the rest of it. This is evidenced every day as Israel demolishes homes, places leaders under house arrest and sets up degrading and protracted checkpoints for Palestinians as Israeli settlers travel freely.

Finally, Jon, as you know, the most damaging misconception has its nexus not in Israel or Palestine, but rather right here in America. Most analysts who speak on the Israeli-Palestinian conflict talk as though our officials in Washington and around the country can be even-handed. The facts are that American politicians and policy makers aid the Israeli military and government to the tune of $5 billion yearly. Israel is the recipient of the largest amount of aid we dole out every year, eating up about one-third of our annual foreign aid budget. How many people could we give health care with that?

4

Jon, stop making me beg, especially when deep down, you're already there. I can gather all the Palestinians I know (it's a lot) and we can have a sit-down.

It'll go something like this:

You: Hi, my name is Jon.
Us: Hi, Jon.
You: And I support justice for Palestinians.
Us: Welcome.

When a Palestinian comedian goes too far

February 18, 2010

Less than a week ago, I was performing at a private party for about 75 Arab-Americans in the suburbs of Detroit. The setting was a restaurant where one half was reserved for this private party while the other half still had regular customers. The side with regular customers was within earshot of my routine. About 3-4 minutes into my act, I told the following joke that I have spoken dozens of times before:

Sometimes I accidentally bring out the racist in people... I don't mean to do it, it just happens. Once, I was sitting in an airport bar because my flight was delayed, not because of me this time. There was this white guy sitting next to me, and since we were both lonely, we started chatting.
He eventually asked me, "What's your name?"
I said, "Amer."
He said, "That's an interesting name... where are you from."
I said, "Well, I grew up in Philly, but now I live in Michigan."
He chuckled and said, "No, I mean, where are you from from?"
This is what white people say when they want to find out where you're REALLY from.
So I said, "Oh, from from... Well, I'm from from Palestine, I'm Palestinian."
And he said, "Really?!"
And I said, "Yeah."
And he said, "REALLY?!?!"
And I said, "Yeah, I didn't say I was a unicorn, I said I'm Palestinian... we exist."
So he looked over both his shoulders, then turned back to me and said, "That's cool... I don't like Jewish people either..."
And so I got upset... I said, "Hey man, that's racist! It's racist of you to assume I'm racist just because of my race... that's racist!"
And he said, "Fine, man, calm down... you mean you don't hate all Jewish people?"

6

And I said, "Well, I'm just sayin..."

And that's the joke.

A couple minutes after I told that, the manager of the restaurant (a complete idiot) came up to me, tugged on my sleeve, and told me, "Don't tell any more jokes about Jewish people, you offended some of my customers." Apparently, some Jewish customers who were not in the private party I was performing for heard the joke and got a little bent out of shape. In the interest of keeping the peace (and since I was performing for a group of people who were going to keep partying long after I left), I simply smiled, assured I would not offend any more customers, and kept performing. I continued and my crowd was having a good time. After about ten minutes, during which time I was squeaky clean and unoffensive, the manager reappeared and asked me to step down. "You've offended everyone," he told me. In shock, I asked, "Who?" He said, "Too many people." I looked at the organizer of the party who invited me, and she did not seem like she wanted to make too big of a deal out of this. So I stepped down. Many attendees of the private party approached me immediately, and expressed their outrage.

Apparently, the few Jewish customers who were offended by the above joke would not stop complaining until I was removed from the stage. Now let me tell you all a little something about that joke. It is not about Jews. It is about some of the incredible things that happen to me as a Palestinian in America. It is about how some white people try to associate with minorities in any way that they can. And finally, it is about how we, as Palestinians and Arab-Americans, sometimes cannot bring ourselves to say we are OK with Jews. At the worst, the joke is offensive to white people and Arabs, but not Jews.

But this is what it means to be Palestinian. You can live anywhere you want, except Palestine, and you can talk about anything you want, except Palestine. You see, the Jews I "offended" that night were not offended by my joke. No, they were offended by the fact that I am Palestinian. They didn't even really hear the joke. They probably heard "Palestinian" and "Jews" and said, "Hey, now wait a minute!"

You see, supporters of Israel are offended by the mere presence of Palestinians, by the mere recital of some sort of Palestinian narrative. In some way, it makes them very uncomfortable. It's kind of like that when you know you're doing something wrong, but you do it anyway. Any Palestinian in

7

the room makes them uneasy. Talking about Israel and its policies makes them edgy. I guess I understand. I'm sure the slaveholders didn't like talking about slavery either.

As Palestinians, our legitimacy depends on whether or not we "recognize" Israel. But supporters of Israel are not required to even acknowledge that Palestinians exist. For an Arab to be taken seriously, he must be "tolerant" of Jews (whatever that means). When a Jew is tolerant of Arabs, he is "open-minded and forward-thinking." At the essence of the Palestinian question lies this complete inequality, this absolute and utter disparity in status. It is almost surreal for the oppressors to be demanding "tolerance" from the oppressed. But it is not without precedent. In America, whites in power demanded that blacks "behave" before they considered "giving" them rights. In South Africa, blacks had to conduct themselves "civilly" before they were taken seriously by the apartheid regime and, indeed, by some powerful political forces here in America.

This sort of calculated framing of the debate by Israel and her supporters serves to silence any Palestinian narrative. Well, guess what? I don't need anyone's permission to be Palestinian. I don't need your go-ahead to tell my story. And you thinking I do kind of pisses me off.

I never wanted that joke to get stale. I was thinking of eventually retiring it. Not anymore.

Is Israel irreplaceable?

Something funny is happening in Israel. There's trouble in paradise.

Last week, on March 10, CNN ran a front-page story on the death of Rachel Corrie. Rachel was killed seven years ago when an Israeli bulldozer crushed her to death while she was protesting the destruction of Palestinian homes in Gaza. Her parents have finally gotten their day in court, as they have sued the Israel's Defense Ministry in connection with their daughter's death. CNN's coverage was related to that occurrence. (Incidentally, Israel has refused to release the name of the driver who killed Rachel, even after clearing him of any wrongdoing).

Things are changing in Israel and America. Not too long ago, this story might have not have made it to the American press at all, as the facts surrounding it make Israel look at best incompetent, or at worst, malicious. American media outlets have made it their stock and trade to shield Israel from such criticism... but things are changing.

Also, on March 9, all major news outlets reported on Vice President Joe Biden's scathing denunciation of Israel's decision to build 1,600 housing units in East Jerusalem. He said that the "substance and timing of the announcement... is precisely the kind of step that undermines the trust we need right now." In the days since then, numerous American officials have echoed his statements, with Secretary of State Hillary Clinton calling the announcement "insulting." Prime Minister Netanyahu has apologized for the timing of the announcement, but has stuck to its substance, saying that building will go forward. Senior White House Advisor David Axelrod fired back, saying the announcement "seemed calculated to undermine" the so-called "proximity talks" the Americans are trying to set up between the parties.

Since this all happened, Palestinians have not been saying much. You know why? Our jaws have fully dropped. We Palestinians have never this seen kind of mudslinging between the Israelis and Americans. And we kinda like it. We've never seen an American administration talk like that to the Israelis. It's pretty cool.

There is no longer that basic unconditional American defense of all Israeli actions, no matter how barbaric or idiotic. The rules are changing. Palestinians are seeing it, and wondering... Is it a dream? Are we on candid camera? Are we getting Punk'd? Well, it's not a dream. This is all happening in a rapidly changing global political hierarchy.

American presidents and politicians have always unequivocally supported Israel, primarily because the strength of the Israeli lobby in the US meant that their unwillingness to do so was (and still may be) political suicide. As American administrations were stoutly supportive of Israel, and since America was the single superpower with no one else even a close second, other nations had to either fall in line or get off Israel's back. That was how we were operating for 60 years.

The collapse of the American economy has changed things. See, we never needed all the other countries before. Now we do. We need China, the EU, India... we need everyone. The field has widened, and America is no longer the undisputed champion. We now need not only the participation of other nations to help us recover, but also their respect. What the current American administration is realizing is that our unwavering support for Israel is something that the rest of the world sees as dim-witted. It is a crutch to dealing with the world on an equal level. While our "special relationship" with Israel was once something the global community of nations had to fully accept, it is now simply an embarrassing hindrance to being taken seriously. In other words, instead of the American position molding the worldview on the subject, it is now the other way around.

Maybe the next step will be for Congress to slash the more than $5 billion we are still giving the Israelis annually. If we seriously want Israel to stop building settlements, we can just stop giving her the money to do it. That $5 billion might better be used right here at home for, well, I don't know, say, healthcare. When it comes to Israel, we hold the purse strings. That's why Palestinians are still wary. While they love seeing America make Israel sleep on the couch, they won't believe the hype until we put our money where our mouth is.

The US has been apologizing for Israel's embarrassing and abusive actions for too long. We give her the money to build the settlements, and then an Israeli politician says that American criticism of settlement policies is meddlesome, uninvited, and "sheer chutzpah." That would be like us trying to dictate things to China if we owed them over $2 trillion. Oh, oops.

We are now having to admit to something we really already knew, that our "unique" relationship with Israel has affected our standing and credibility with everyone else. Well, we can't be Israel's battered spouse anymore. We're going on Oprah! We want our life back! We're dumping you! It's time to call the cops, and this time, we're pressing charges! Israel, to the left, to the left!

Maybe Palestine can catch America on the rebound... and you know what they say about Palestinian guys... well, that's for another day.

The great democracy of Israel

June 1, 2010

Israel attacked (not surrounded, not redirected... attacked) a ship bringing supplies to Gaza, which has been blockaded by Israel for 3 years now. Why did Israel blockade Gaza? Because she was unhappy with the democratic decision of its people to elect Hamas to power.

Israel, the only democracy in the Middle East.

Israel arrested two Palestinians, who are Israeli citizens by the way, Omar Said and Ameer Makhoul, and she then proceeded to accuse them of spying for Hizbollah. Makhoul was denied access to a lawyer for 2 weeks following his arrest. Makhoul and Said are prominent human rights activists, working inside Israel. Israel has still not presented any evidence against them. Why did Israel arrest them? Because she was not happy with what they were saying. Both Makhoul and Said have been deprived the most basic fundamental legal rights. Their real crime is being Palestinian in Israel.

Israel, the only democracy in the Middle East.

Israel's official languages are both Arabic and Hebrew. Recently, however, Israel has started to change the names of Arab cities on street signs, replacing their Arabic names with their Hebrew names, transliterated into Arabic. For instance, when describing Jerusalem, instead of writing "al-Quds" in Arabic (its correct name in Arabic), they are now writing "Yerushalim" in Arabic (its Hebrew name). I know, this does not make sense to normal people like you and me. But Israel isn't normal. It's not as if the next generation of Palestinians will stop calling it "al-Quds." We've been calling it that for a pretty long time. But Israel is simply doing what it has been trying to do since before 1948: eradicate any sense of Arabness in Palestine. This might work... except... oops, Israel still has more than 5 million Arabs under its control.

Israel, the only democracy in the Middle East.

Jewish towns and roads are generously pumped with government money, while Arab ones are left to languish with no help. Jews are granted building permits with no hassle, while Arabs must jump through numerous hoops in hopes of even securing one. Infant mortality among Arab citizens of Israel is two and a half times higher than it is among Jews. 50% of

Israeli Arab college graduates are out of work. Arabs make up 6% of the civil service, but are 18% of the country's citizens. Arab elementary and middle school students trail Jewish pupils in math, science, and English, and the gap is widening. Arabs suffer much more poverty, and the national education system spends considerably more per Jewish child than per Arab child. I haven't even talked about the Law of Return, which grants any Jew in the world automatic citizenship to Israel while denying the rights of Palestinians living inside Israel, the West Bank, Gaza, and elsewhere. To Israel, being Palestinian simply means one thing: You can live anywhere in the world you want... except here.

Benjamin Netanyahu, the leader of the Middle East's only democracy, told us that the activists on the flotilla boat "deliberately attacked" the Israeli soldiers who were dropped from helicopters onto their ship in international waters. Wait a second... the Israeli commandos undertook a surprise attack on a ship full of unarmed activists, then got "deliberately attacked?" That's like saying, "A burglar broke into Amer's house... then Amer proceeded to deliberately kick his ass." Maybe in Middle Eastern democracies, "deliberately attacked" means something different than it does in America.

In our democratic America, our leaders have spent the last 24 hours doing damage control, trying to keep strong language out of the UN Security Council's resolution condemning the attack. President Obama, we have bigger things to worry about. When they ask you about Israel, just say "No comment... I got a hole in the Gulf of Mexico, the economy is shit, and they're rounding up Latinos in Arizona... I can't deal with that crazy bitch Israel right now." Israel is like our alcoholic friend... she always get wasted, does something really stupid, then we apologize for her... "Sorry guys, Israel was so drunk last night... she usually doesn't kill activists in public like that."

Except she does. Israel is much more scared of international human rights organizations like Free Gaza than she has ever been of Hamas. If Hamas does something counter to Israeli interests, Israel can simply bomb them, kill a few innocent bystanders, apologize, and move on. But non-violence is something Israel has no idea how to deal with. Branding as terrorists those who challenge Israel in a non-violent manner is nothing new. Edward Said, Noam Chomsky, Hanan Ashrawi, they have all gone through this. Killing those who use their intellect to confront and defy Israel is nothing new for

13

her either. Simply ask the families of Naji el-Ali and Ghassan Kanafani.

In the Middle East's only democracy, democracy is dead. Or more accurately, it was never alive.

Oh, Helen, behave!

December 10, 2010

Helen, don't you know that you can't say the Jews should get the hell out of Palestine? Don't you know it's not even called Palestine? Don't you know that there never was a Palestine?

C'mon, Helen...

Don't you know you can't talk about the extreme bias in American media in favor of Israel? Don't you know there is no bias? Don't you know that Israel shares our American values?

Helen, seriously...

Don't you know you can't piss off the pro-Israel lobbies by speaking of Israeli aggression, law breaking, discrimination, bullying, lying, manipulation, collective punishment, indiscriminate killing, dispossession, illegal land grabbing, occupation, and apartheid?

Well, maybe you didn't bring all those things up, but it sure seems like it.

You would think that after working all those years in Washington you would know what you can say and what you can't. But then again, maybe that's why you did it. Maybe you just got sick of it all, and when that guy shoved that camera in your face, you just thought to yourself, "Screw it, I'll just say the Jews should get the hell out of Palestine."

The constant browbeating had finally been enough. Murmurs in the White House press corps that you were a Hizbollah operative or a Hamas informant had finally gotten to you. The idea that an Arab was even lucky to be there finally became unbearable.

See, as you know Helen, we Arab-Americans, and Palestinians especially, usually need to ask permission to tell our story. The Palestinian narrative can never be introduced without an opposing Israeli view, in order to be "fair." Of course, pro-Israeli views are often broadcast without any such need for rebuttal. The baseline assumption is that the Palestinian narrative is biased, in need of the Israelis to balance it out. The Israeli narrative, on the other hand, is fully respectful of the truth.

Never mind that pro-Israeli advocates are Picasso-esque in their artistry of lying. Sometimes it looks like a lie, sometimes

15

it doesn't, but it always is. And even when it's obvious, it still works. I remember always seeing them on the Sunday talk shows. The Israeli guy would say, "The Palestinians attacked us first." And the Palestinian guy would yell, "You're lying!!" And the Israeli guy would calmly respond, "Yes, but let me finish."

Helen, on December 2 in Dearborn, Michigan, you said, "Congress, the White House, Hollywood, Wall Street are owned by the Zionists."

People got upset and Wayne State University discontinued an award in your name. They said you were anti-Semitic. For saying Jews own all the important stuff? As Arabs, we don't get the anger. If someone said we owned those things, we'd take the credit. Or at least we'd say, "Well we don't own it yet, but we're working on it."

I don't know if Zionists own all those things, but it sure does seem like it.

If you mean that Congress is pro-Zionist, you might have a point. $160 billion in foreign aid to Israel does seem pretty lovey-dovey.

If you mean the White House is pro-Zionist, I can see where you're coming from. Visits by American presidential candidates to Israeli towns as part of their routine campaign stops does seem kind of cuddly-cuddly.

If you mean Hollywood is pro-Zionist, you might have a point. *True Lies, Rules of Engagement,* and *Delta Force* all portray Arabs as violent, stupid terrorists. And to make things worse, the most prominent Arab in Hollywood is Paula Abdul. Just once it would be ok with me for her tell people she's Mexican. But her last name just has to be Abdul. Dammit! Barely anyone knows Tony Shalhoub is Arab, but he is!! He is!

And Wall Street? I don't know about that one. Unless you put it in terms of gas and cigarette prices, most of us will never understand that place. But if you say it's pro-Zionist, I'll go with it.

But Helen, you have to be careful. Pro-Israel advocates equate criticism (or sometimes mere talk) of Zionism with racism against Jews. Zionism equals Judaism, they say. Sure, it doesn't seem to make sense, but it sure does work. Even we Arabs have become victims of this distorted rationalization, turning into schizophrenics whenever anyone asks us how we feel.

Do you hate Jews? OF COURSE NOT!

16

Do you like Jews? OF COURSE NOT!

But you almost make it sound like the Zionists control everything. It seems preposterous, although I do remember being in Ramallah, getting lost, pressing home on my GPS machine, then hearing Benjamin Netanyahu's voice say, "You no longer live in that house anymore."

But Helen, can you really blame the White House and Congress for being so blatantly pro-Israel? They know they need to tow the Israeli line, or else they'll end up like you, being the ones who need to get the hell out.

My Christmas gift to Israel

December 27, 2010

For Palestinians, Christmas is very special. We're related to Jesus. My family is from Nazareth, and I'm pretty sure they're direct descendants of some of Mary's cousins. Wait, that means if you go back far enough, I'm a Jew. Man, that really confuses the anti-Semitic side of me. But I'm adding it to my résumé anyway. That should help me at the border next time I visit.

Actually, my dad's side of the family came to Nazareth from Syria in the 1700s, and my mom's side came there from Egypt about a hundred years before that. I guess the Israelis are right... we're not really from there... Dammit.

But that doesn't necessarily mean I'm not a Jew. See, many of the families (tribes) in Palestine, if you go back far enough, were Jewish, and later converted to Christianity or Islam. Sometimes, Jews converted to Christianity, then Islam. Pretty confusing. And while you convert to Christianity or Islam, you never stop being a Jew, because that's genetic. Rabbis say that as long as you were born to a Jewish woman (even if she's not a self-described Jew at the time), you're a Jew. There's no conversion out. So basically, all the Palestinians who were originally Jews are only now impersonating Christians and Muslims. I only needed one of those impostors to marry into my lineage, and presto: I'm a Jew.

So Israel, I'm probably a Jew. Merry Christmas!

And to my newly found brethren, I have another gift. I'm done being confused! See, as a young Palestinian kid in America, Christmas really accentuated my differences. I remember going to the mall and seeing Santa. He would ask me, "What do you want for Christmas, little boy?" And I would say, "GI Joe, a Huffy bike, and the enforcement of UN Resolution 242." It turns out Santa's not real.

But luckily, I don't need him to be. My gift to my Jewish brethren is a new strategy for us Palestinians. It has three steps:

1. We abandon our claim to a Palestinian state.
2. We stop all violence.
3. We wait.

18

We don't need a state. You already declared one for us sixty years ago. We're happy, with our newly found commonalities, to be part of the one that's already there. It seems to be working pretty well. Once we all get accurately recognized as Jews, things should be just fine. But can we change the name? "Israel" has brand recognition, but it's not all good. You know, the massacres, the military occupation, and whatnot. I was thinking... "Palestine." I know that might be touchy, but it does have a certain ring to it. Now we will have to conduct thorough testing, as there are some people in Palestine who don't have the necessary Jewish lineage that I probably do. We need to find out who they are. But we're not kicking them out. We did that once, and it caused major problems. After we find out who they are, they will stay, and we will marry them all to Jewish women as quickly as possible. In a generation or two, the problem is solved. We need to make as many as Palestinian Jews as possible. And we're better than the ones from Russia and Ethiopia. We come with land.

Palestinians must stop all aggression. The reasoning here is clear and concise. I simply don't believe in Jew-on-Jew violence. We need to be united.

Finally, we Palestinians will wait. Surely, there will be some people in our society who might not accept our newly found Jewishness. We can wait them out. If Jewish history has taught us anything, it's that we are capable of waiting. Eventually, they'll come around.

We need to make a few more changes to complete everything. Since it was Jesus's birthday that brought about this revelation, Palestine's Independence Day will be December 25. Until now, Palestinian Independence Day has been on April 1, and that's just mean.

So, Merry Christmas, Happy Independence Day, and Happy New Year! And when someone can explain Hanukah to me, I'll start celebrating that too!

Santa Claus, the Easter bunny, & the Palestinians

January 3, 2011

One of the perils in writing about the Palestine/Israel question is that one can sometimes be misunderstood. There are so many nuances that when one writes in a fashion outside the normal lines of the debate, he might receive the same criticism and praise from all sides.

Last week, I wrote a satirical column about how we Palestinians could rediscover our lost "Jewishness" and become citizens of Israel. I also claimed that Santa Claus wasn't real since he never got me what I really wanted for Christmas: justice for the Palestinians. I then received some furious responses:

> *E-mail from a Jew: Amer, how dare you say you want to be a citizen of Israel?!*
> *E-mail from an Arab: Amer, how dare you say you want to be a citizen of Israel?!*
> *E-mail from Santa Claus: Amer, maybe next year. Oh, and the Easter Bunny says hello.*

When I wrote my last column, I was being, um, how do you say, sarcastic. A mass Palestinian conversion to Judaism would of course solve nothing, since Israel's moniker as a Jewish state has very little to do with actually being Jewish, and much more to do with being a colonial-settler project. That is to say Israel is much less concerned with what it brought to the land of Palestine, and much more concerned with eliminating what was already there. Israel, in its own eyes, can never fully succeed unless it rids itself of its "Palestinian-ness."

Israel has always had this nagging problem: us. See, it turns out that "a land without a people for a people without a land" actually wasn't true. I can imagine that if it were, we may have never seen Ethiopian, Iranian, Iraqi, and Russian Jews (and non-Jews) brought into Israel. Israel has always seen herself as fighting a demographic war. Moreover, she has propagated this massive myth that somehow the Jews are the "natives" and the Palestinians the "foreigners." This is

20

how Israel gets away with talking about "tolerating" the Palestinian presence.

In this sense, it is not much different from early American settlement activity, which came to see itself existing only in opposition to the native population, first undertaking policies to wipe them all out, then creating a society in which they were essentially non-persons, or even worse, a "nuisance." In fact, on the 2010 Census form, the term "Native American" is not even used. It instead uses "American Indian," a term that is inaccurate, and most importantly, does not connote that these people in fact had a preexisting tie to the land we all live on today. This kind of talk might disturb and confuse most Americans, and, frankly, ruin the myths we have been taught. In fact, I would love to go to the next major Republican gathering and ask all the Native Americans to identify themselves. I think Sarah Palin might raise her hand.

Palestinians are ready for peace. Let me tell you how I know this to be certain. Some time ago, even before the laughable 1993 Oslo Accords, Palestinians far and wide fully came to accept that whatever solution is ultimately reached would include our living, breathing, and working alongside Jewish Israelis in everyday life. Conversely, high-ranking Jewish leaders and politicians are still, in 2011, having discussions about how to get rid of the Palestinians.

Well Israel, let me tell you something that many of your neighboring countries already know. We're bad houseguests. We don't leave when you ask us to. Except... oh, yeah... we're not guests in Israel. You are. But you know what, you can stay as long as you like... forever even. We Palestinians should adopt a new strategy, being the first society in the last 500 years to tell Jews that they are completely welcome. Of course, the last society to do that was also Arab and Muslim. Jews lived freely in Muslim and Arab empires, economically, religiously, intellectually, and politically. So with open arms, we accept you. I know, Hamas is being a little bitchy, but let me talk to them. They'll come around.

But Israel, you have to accept us too. We're not going anywhere. Unlike Santa Claus and the Easter Bunny, we actually exist.

Gaza...

January 19, 2011

It was two years ago that Israel was completing her invasion into Gaza. Over 1400 Palestinians were killed, over half of them civilians. In most other parts of the world, anniversaries are something to celebrate. Not in Gaza. Israel finally withdrew, after deciding that further incursions would be politically disastrous. She always seems to know just how much she can get away with.

Palestinians, and many human rights groups, decried the invasion as too heavy-handed, disproportionate, and indifferent to civilian safety. But no international action was taken. Those Israelis always seem to know just how much they can get away with.

Gaza is many times referred to as "one of the most densely populated places on the planet." Israel's supporters have refuted that claim. And you know... they're right. There are hundreds of places that are more densely populated than Gaza. In fact, via a quick Google search I found a sermon by Rabbi Leigh Lerner where he noted, among other things, that the city of Montreal, where he lives, is more densely populated than Gaza:

> *The fact is, the population density of Gaza is not out of line with urban areas elsewhere. The density is less than Montreal's. The constant reiteration that Gaza is one of the most densely populated places on earth is one more way of convincing the world that the Palestinian refugees are in a cage created by Israel. Does anyone in Montreal think this city is a cage? There seems to be enough room for everyone, indeed, room to spare, and we have more people per square kilometer than Gaza.*

The rabbi must know that the Palestinians in Gaza are indeed in a cage, and that it was indeed created by Israel. This is not up for debate. He must know that the main difference between the inhabitants of Gaza and the citizens of Montreal is that the latter can actually leave if they want to. And then come back, and then leave again, and so forth. In other words, they are free. Rabbi Lerner too knows exactly what he can get away with.

In the Gaza War of 2008, Israel started with a massive air offensive. She struck about 200 targets in the first few hours, including killing a couple dozen young men at a police graduation ceremony. In all, on that first day, 230 Palestinians were killed and over 700 injured. Israel dropped American-made bombs using American-made F-16 jets and American-made Apache helicopters. Maybe next time she can drop other American stuff, like hamburgers, apple pies, and the cast of "Jersey Shore." The guys in Gaza would love Snookie.

The IDF admittedly targeted the houses of Hamas leaders, with full knowledge that the rest of their family members were present. They got away with that too.

Israel says it dropped leaflets to warn residents in high-risk areas to flee before an airstrike occurred. If you've never been to Gaza, you can easily find out what it's like. Go to a Wal-Mart on a Sunday afternoon when it's really packed. Then imagine they lock all the doors. Then imagine they only turn on the water and electricity for a few hours a day. A few of the members of this new Wal-Mart community might go crazy. You might not agree with the crazies, but you know why they're crazy. Then the same people who locked the doors tell you all to stop being so crazy. You organize demonstrations, chanting, "Unlock the doors!" They respond by attacking you all, to root out all the "crazies." And they're still not unlocking the doors. But lucky for you, they drop leaflets. "Attention Wal-Mart shoppers... We will be bombing the Sporting Goods department in 15 minutes. We hope no flying bikes hit you in the head."

I never understood this leaflet-dropping nonsense. If you say you're targeting terrorists, and then drop leaflets to warn the non-terrorists, won't the terrorists see the leaflets too? Are the terrorists illiterate? Or maybe the leaflet asks the non-terrorists not to tell the terrorists. Of course, none of Israel's actions are about getting the terrorists. In this military campaign, as with her other campaigns, her objective was to punish those whom she has imprisoned, precisely for speaking out against their imprisonment. She knows exactly what she can get away with.

This is why true debate on the Palestinian-Israeli conflict, at least when it includes people like Rabbi Lerner, can go nowhere. It's easy to lie when you know there will be no consequences. It's easy to say and do things that are ridiculously

23

illogical when you have seen you can get away with it so easily.

Now that I think of it, I have some shopping to do this weekend. I hear Wal-Mart is having an anniversary sale this Sunday. I think I'll go. But I'd still rather be in Gaza.

Israel's new Sarah

May 13, 2011

A few weeks ago, I returned from a month-long trip in Palestine, where I put on some comedy shows, ate too much hummus (yes, that's possible), and witnessed the general ridiculousness of the Palestinian-Israeli conflict. As it turns out, however, I was not the most famous American in the region at the time. Sarah Palin was also visiting the Holy Land. I'm not sure whether she was there to see me or to see Jesus, but either way, we Arabs love visitors.

But she wasn't there for us. I'm sure many of you saw the photos of her touring around Jerusalem with her Israeli tour guides, wearing a Star of David on her necklace, visiting the Temple Mount, and talking about how much she loves Israel. And I'm also sure you all remember how she drove up the checkpoint to enter Bethlehem, only to abruptly turn around right before entering the Palestinian-controlled area. What a tease!

I would not normally pick on Sarah Palin too much. She rarely crosses my radar. But her visit to Israel reminded me of some things she has said in the past. It is no secret that supporters of Israel in America are trained with talking points, and they use them incessantly.

Palin once had the following exchange with Barbara Walters:

Palin: I believe the Jewish settlements should be allowed to be expanded upon... and I don't think that the Obama administration has any right to tell Israel that the Jewish settlements cannot expand.
Walters: Even if it's Palestinian areas?
Palin: I believe that the Jewish settlements should be allowed to expand.

And the following conversation with Charlie Gibson:

Gibson: What if Israel decided it felt threatened and needed to take out the Iranian nuclear facilities?
Palin: I don't think we should second-guess the measures Israel has to take to defend itself and for their security.

25

Gibson: So if we wouldn't second-guess and they decided they needed to do it because Iran was an existential threat, we would be cooperative or agree with that?

Palin: I don't think we can second-guess what Israel has to do to secure its nation.

Gibson: So if it felt necessary, if it felt the need, to defend itself, by taking out an Iranian nuclear facility, that would be all right?

Palin: We cannot second-guess the steps Israel has to take to defend itself.

I'm not exactly sure how the Israel lobby trains its spokespeople. I'm not allowed in the meetings. But I guess it goes something like, "Just say the same thing 3 times in a row, no matter what the question is... works every time." Even Sarah Palin can remember a simple rule like that. I understand the strategy. When you're uttering complete bullshit, it's important to stay on point.

It works like this:

Wife: Did you forget our anniversary?
Husband: I love you honey.
Wife: How could you forget?
Husband: Baby, I love you so much...
Wife: I could just kill you!
Husband: I love you more than anything.
Wife: Aww, I love you too.

Now, Sarah Palin is rarely worthy of much intellectual conversation, so I'll do my best to avoid any. But I can at least say, "Sarah, stick to guns, abortion, and hockey... leave Palestine and Israel to me." I know she's running for president, and everyone knows that during a presidential campaign, Israel suddenly becomes the 51st state, with candidates scrambling to campaign there. I can handle Sarah Palin when she talks about everything else. But when she starts talking about me, I start to get pissed off.

In all seriousness, I thought she was the super-Christian. For all her talk about Jesus, it's weird that a few Arabs would scare her off from visiting his crib. Seriously, Sarah, there's nothing to be scared of. We Palestinians love white women, and we're used to seeing them with guns pointed at us. You would have felt right at home.

But I'll tell you this, Sarah. As a Palestinian, I can sleep well each and every night, because I know if Jesus were around today, he'd be on my side. And he'd be my cousin too. Yeah, that's right.

Jesus is my cousin.
Jesus is my cousin.
Jesus is my cousin.

May 15, and we're still surviving...

May 16, 2011

It's May 15. Israeli Independence Day. Nakba Day. Israelis "celebrate" this day. We Palestinians "commemorate" it. "Celebrate" and "commemorate" mean entirely different things. As Americans, we "celebrate" July 4. We "commemorate" September 11.

Without getting into too much detail (which, I'll tell you, is painfully difficult for a Palestinian), May 15, 1948 marked the creation of the Israeli state. It also marked the commencement of the world's longest-running policy of ethnic cleansing. The state of Israel is nothing if not persistent.

About 70% of Palestinians live outside of Palestine. And we're successful everywhere we go. There's nothing special in our DNA. We just don't have a "Plan B."

We've always had to struggle. We are notoriously hard workers. And we don't take vacations. It's not because we wouldn't like to lie on a sunny beach somewhere. We just don't like leaving our houses for more than a couple days. We remember what happened last time we did that.

As a Palestinian, I am angry at Israel. It's not because she steals our land and houses. I'm sure we'll figure all that out one day. It's not because she kills us indiscriminately. We're good at reproduction. (Incidentally, for all those non-Palestinian women who don't know, we're also very good at "practicing" reproduction.)

I'm mad for the same reason my first girlfriend was mad at me... because Israel is a damn liar!

They are masterful at it, of course. Israel makes Richard Nixon, Bill Clinton, and George W. Bush look like amateurs. Israel is the Kaiser Soze of nations, convincingly fabricating history and making everyone believe it.

Israel's compulsion for fibbing started with what has now become her most famous lie, namely that Palestine was "a land without a people, for a people without a land."

It must be said neither Jews nor Israelis coined this slogan. But it wouldn't be the first time Israel has stolen something and used it for her own benefit.

28

This lie has always especially pissed me off. The "people without a land" part is easy enough to swallow. But "a land without a people?"

Israel, I know you've been trying to deny our existence forever, but seriously, no one believes you anymore. The party is over.

If Palestine was a land without a people, who lived in the 400 villages you destroyed in 1948?

If Palestine was a land without a people, who are those millions of stateless people living in those 59 UN refugee camps, going to the schools with the blue-framed windows?

If Palestine was a land without a people, who lived in Akka, Safad, and Eilabun? Who lived in Deir Yassin?

If Palestine was a land without a people, why are you smoking hookahs, saying "yalla," and eating hummus?

See, I don't care that the Israelis want to live in Palestine. But I do care when they pretend that we don't exist. If Israel wants to make hummus, that's fine with me. I had some Israel hummus last time I was there. It was delicious. They learned well. Hey, we make a lot more pizza here in America than Italians do in Italy. But at least we have the decency to put an Italian flag on front of the shop.

Israel is pretending like we were never present. It's still pretending that she arrived upon a "land without a people." It's very annoying. I know now how a lady feels when she sleeps with a guy, sees him a couple days later, and he totally ignores her. Ladies, I feel your pain. Israel gave me the old "wham bam thank you ma'am."

So every May 15, we remember what Israel did. And Israel doesn't like it. Today, Israel killed 12 Palestinians on the borders of Lebanon and Syria. They died because they dared to remind her that they still exist.

On this Nakba Day, though, I am not sad. Every Palestinian walking the earth today, whether in Ramallah, Lebanon, America, or Australia, is basically a survivor of Israel's attempts to wipe us, and everything about us, off of the face of the earth.

So, to my fellow Palestinians I say... Congratulations! We've lasted another year, and we show no signs of surrender. Israel, just accept us already. Your plan to exterminate us failed. It's time to throw in the towel. Nakba Day is now "Survival Day."

"A land without a people?!" Then who the hell am I?

Thanks to Israel, I didn't forget. Each Palestinian knows what his particular history of displacement is. Each feels that attachment to a shared experience, provided by Israel, which binds us all together. As a Palestinian, I wake up daily, with a hole in my heart. And I try to fill it... by eating as much hummus as I can.

Bibi, Barack, & recognition

May 24, 2011

As a Palestinian-American, I have spent the last week glued to my television set. The Palestinian-Israeli saga has been in headlines daily. After over 60 years, even tornadoes, floods and volcanoes can't stop us. It seems that God is trying his best to rip us from the headlines, but it's not working.

Presidential policy outlines, speeches to AIPAC, and an address to Congress by the Israeli Prime Minister are like crack to me. I've been unable to turn off the news for a week. For a Palestinian, that's not saying much. While some people invite their friends over to watch a movie, we're a little different. "Hey Jihad, I just made some popcorn... Wanna come over and watch Anderson Cooper?" Yes, we watch CNN too much... and yes, sometimes we name our kids Jihad.

Of course, there was not much new in the news, at least not for us. It was simply the same old love-fest between American politicians and Israel. Barack Obama, like the 5 presidents before him, is trying his best to bring the ultimate peace. And like them, he will be unsuccessful.

See, what President Obama does not understand is that the Palestinian-Israeli peace process is not about Palestinians recognizing Israel's right to exist. It is about exactly the opposite.

Israel has been attempting to rid herself of the Palestinians since her inception. Village massacres in the 1948 war, racist government policies, and settlement building on occupied Palestinian land have been some of the methods Israel has implemented in trying to achieve this goal.

We don't need to recognize Israel. Israel needs to recognize us.

In 1993, the PLO (the sole representative of the Palestinian people at the time) recognized Israel's right to exist. But Israeli politicians, cabinet members, and Benjamin Netanyahu still talk about ridding themselves of the Palestinian "demographic threat."

We don't need to recognize Israel. Israel needs to recognize us.

After the 1993 Oslo Accords (which were approved in a manner much more beneficial to Israel's interests than to the

31

Palestinians'), Palestinians went on to build a quasi-governmental authority in an attempt to move forward in a process that would ultimately allow them to govern themselves. Yasser Arafat was received as a hero, though admittedly he was nothing of the sort. Yitzhak Rabin's prize for attempting to make peace with the Palestinians was his assassination at the hands of one of his own Jewish citizens.

We don't need to recognize Israel. Israel needs to recognize us.

And I really hate to keep harping on this, but hummus is not Israeli. Israeli hummus makers can keep making hummus. I just ask that they place a little disclaimer on the container: "Recipe originally Palestinian."

In what world is it sane to call the indigenous people of a land a "demographic threat?" This is not about how far back you want to go in history. This is not about who was there first. This is just about who was there. Palestinians are a reality that Israel still does not want to accept.

Israel has implemented its ethnic cleansing policies at a very slow rate. They are clearly patient. But patience is supposed to ultimately yield positive results. For Israel, that positive result is the expulsion of the native Palestinian population. And it's not working. Israel sees that, and is clearly bothered by that reality. The whole Israeli-Palestinian conflict revolves not around land. Nor is it centered on differing beliefs in the divine. It is simply about a population in power trying to expel a less powerful one from the same land.

After President Obama declared that a settlement should be based on the 1967 borders, Netanyahu went crazy (or crazier). He declared those borders "indefensible." We should of course remember that Israel fought the 1967 war against Jordan, Egypt, and Syria. As a result, it occupied the Gaza Strip from Egypt, the West Bank from Jordan, and the Golan Heights from Syria. Syria still lays claim to the Golan Heights (which would not be incorporated into a Palestinian state in any case), but Jordan and Egypt, with whom Israel now enjoys peace agreements, no longer lay any claim to Gaza or the West Bank. So against what threat exactly are these borders "indefensible?"

Israel has injected about 500,000 illegal settlers into the West Bank and East Jerusalem. Israel does not want to negotiate about these areas. See, Netanyahu lashed out at President Obama precisely because he does want to negotiate with the Palestinians, a people he sees as having no claim to the land they live upon.

32

We don't need to recognize Israel. Israel needs to recognize us.

President Obama, of course, quickly apologized in a speech a few days later to the American Israel Public Affairs Committee (AIPAC). He reiterated that "1967 borders" actually meant "1967 borders with mutually agreed upon land swaps," and in any case did not include East Jerusalem. Jerusalem would remain "undivided." He received thunderous applause.

The next day, Netanyahu addressed Congress saying exactly the same thing. He also received thunderous applause, this time from American lawmakers, who have never shown their own president that same level of enthusiasm. In other words, "1967 borders" means absolutely nothing. It means whatever Israel wants it to mean. And if the pesky Palestinians complain, they are an "obstacle to peace."

What Obama and Netanyahu need to understand and acknowledge is that the Palestinians actually exist. We're not going anywhere. Only when Israel recognizes that essential fact can there be real discussions on how to move forward. We are not a "demographic threat." We are a "demographic reality." We are rightful inhabitants. We deserve security. We have good values. We have a culture, a history, and a narrative.

We exist. Recognize that.

We can't split the baby in half

June 1, 2011

The Israeli-Palestinian marriage is reaching a monumental tipping point. With a right-wing Israeli government that has basically told the world it does not want to see any sort of Palestinian state, and a Palestinian leadership bent on declaring a non-effectual state in September, we are at a point where fate might just have to kick in.

I make no mistake in referring to the Israelis and the Palestinians as a married couple. Sure, it was a marriage forced upon them, perhaps by God, perhaps by history, perhaps by the British (those pesky British). In any case, it is a marriage that can only result in either the survival or demise of both spouses. There can be no winner, and both must realize this sobering reality.

The reason there can be no winner is because there is a child. The land of Palestine is a baby that cannot be cut in half. If the 63-year old Israeli enterprise has proved anything, it is that the Israeli state cannot exist as one that is both Jewish and democratic. It can also not exist as long as it consciously denies it Palestinian-Arab character.

We Palestinians are exasperating. We have not left, deserted our culture, or abandoned our language. And we have not forgotten.

But it should be noted that the Palestinians have absolutely nothing to offer in any sort of peace negotiations. Sure, we can promise things, but that's about it. No Palestinian leader, however, has anything tangible to offer Israel. Any "final settlement" will be on Israel's terms only.

So Israel will have to make a monumental choice that will basically boil down to either becoming fully Jewish or fully democratic. She has for 63 years attempted to become fully Jewish. She has failed. Perhaps it is time to try the democratic option. But becoming democratic is not an undertaking that can be done halfway, or in a manner that ignores 5 million people. Being democratic is like being pregnant. You either are or you aren't.

A single-state solution has been thrown about by Palestinians and Israelis alike. Most argue for it on humanist and moral grounds. And there is no doubt that such a solution would, in principle, solve many of those problems. But there are much bigger reasons to pursue the single state.

Let's start with the economy. Does anyone truly understand what sort of economic treasure exists for us? Some nations have oil, some have technology, and some have beaches. We have God. And while those other things might run out someday, God, if history tells us anything, is not going anywhere. If the land of Palestine were opened up to the whole world, a thousand hotels would need to be built. Can you imagine how much money would flow if Muslims around the world could visit? Yes, I know it scares Israel. But I'm not talking about the Muslims you see on CNN. I'm talking about the other 99.9%, the ones that would visit Jerusalem, Nazareth, Bethlehem, Hebron, and everywhere else. Believe it or not, they have money. I can only dream of the amount of money Saudi princes alone would spend in Jerusalem. Imagine if the Lebanese border opened up. Sure, we might have to build a plastic surgery complex somewhere in Palestine, but the Lebanese would spend a lot of money too! Palestine could become a Holy Disney. As long as Israel remains cut off from 300 million Arabs and over one billion Muslims, billions of dollars are being lost.

We must all also come to terms with another reality. If you ask a Palestinian to draw his country, he traces that triangle the British made for us long ago. It is that triangle from which we draw our identity. We don't leave out Jerusalem, Nazareth, Haifa, and Yafa. But there's a funny thing. If you ask an Israeli to draw his country, he draws the same thing. That's why Gaza and the West Bank are still occupied. Israel has no intention of giving up the land, or giving up the baby. She just doesn't want to recognize Palestinian parental rights as well. But we are there, constantly reminding Israel of it, much to her dismay. But I must tell the Israelis one thing, and it might shock them. There is a reason you eat hummus, smoke hookahs, and throw around Arabic slang. Your baby, whether you like it or not, is half Palestinian.

And the baby cannot be cut in half. We're talking about the same place, the same land. We're not talking about borders that will come down nicely neatly separating populations from each other. Attempting to draw borders in order to split the baby is a pointless endeavor. Let's just stick with the ones white people drew for us after World War I. Those are the borders within which Palestinians define themselves. They are the exact same borders within which Israel controls all entry and exit today. There will be no successful agreement unless a one-state solution is implemented.

Both Israelis and Palestinians want the whole baby. And both can have it. But the Palestinians, as the battered and forgotten spouse, will have no say. The whole future hinges on Israel finally acknowledging that she has failed in trying to rid herself of us. A sustainable, profitable, and respectable future can only be realized when Israel accepts that Palestinians are worthy of the same humanity and respect that Jews are. The baby can then have two healthy parents. And like most older Jewish and Arab couples, they will stay married, falling asleep each night in the same house... in separate bedrooms.

BEWARE... Being Palestinian is contagious

July 16, 2011

Last weekend, I was lucky enough to perform at the annual convention of the American Federation of Ramallah Palestine in Washington, DC. I saw many old friends and met many new ones. I performed in three comedy shows, and I can tell you this: Palestinians know how to laugh, especially at themselves. But I also confirmed something else I always suspected to be true... Being Palestinian is contagious!

I met a few couples at the gathering that were, for lack of a better word, mixed. Palestinians are spread all over the world. Being Palestinian basically means you can live anywhere except Palestine. As a result, we have more mixed marriages than any other species on earth. In America alone, we have occupied over 5 million non-Palestinians. OK, I don't know if that number is exactly accurate, but it happens a lot.

I met one particular white guy, let's call him Mark, who married a Palestinian woman. During one of my shows, I asked his father-in-law how he could let such a thing happen. It turns out his daughter was 33 when she married Mark, so that explains a lot. When single Arab women pass the age of 25, their parents tend to stop being too particular.

When I asked Mark where his wife was, I noticed he was surrounded by Arab men on either side. As he identified his wife seated two chairs away from him, I discovered that his brother-in-law was sitting between him and his wife. I'm sure his brother-in-law was present on their first date, so I guess old habits die hard.

In my comedy travels, I frequently meet white guys married to Palestinian women, and what I have noticed is that they have been "Palestinianized." They love hummus, speak loudly, and march in demonstrations. They eat grape leaves, wear keffiyehs, and can recite UN Resolutions 194 and 242. They give their kids Arabic names, love garlic, and have pictures of Jerusalem in their homes. We have infected them. In a good way.

Being Palestinian is cool. We Palestinians love it, so it's no wonder we rub off on others so easily. Incidentally, I have never seen the opposite happen. I have never witnessed a Palestinian marry a white American only to start suddenly saying "dude," liking Sarah Palin, and over-indulging in mayonnaise.

I have rubbed off on many people over the years. I've had a few white girlfriends, and if they didn't know about Palestine before they dated me, they sure did after. It has caused some uncomfortable moments. I remember when Britney and Ashley both showed up to that anti-Israeli demonstration a few years ago... Awkward.

Being Palestinian is relentless. Every Palestinian has a story. Our stories and personal histories tell of our collective struggle. And once non-Palestinians have drunk the potion, there is no cure.

No Palestinian can claim to be independent of our history. No Palestinian can escape it. To live a life divorced from political reality is impossible for any Palestinian. We are consumed by history even before birth. Our greatest achievement is our abiding refusal to become casualties. When non-Palestinians join the club, they quickly realize that membership is not just a matter of eating too much garlic. It comes with an acute political memory unlike any other. I'm sure many white guys remember their first meeting with their prospective Palestinian father-in-law. After he served coffee and said hello, the next words out of his mouth were, "In 1948..."

After hearing that talk, you have caught the bug. But all in all, it's a pretty good bug to catch. The symptoms aren't all that bad...

You will start overeating. White people can eat small meals and be satisfied. We eat meals in phases. We even take breaks. You will find yourself running to the dinner table, and limping away from it.

You will redefine the word "cousin." For us, it can mean a first cousin, a third cousin five times removed, or even just a friend. It can also mean a wife.

You will find that you start dancing in circular line formations at weddings and celebrations. You will stomp on the floor and sweat profusely. Relatives that you didn't know you had will grab your hand and lead you in the right direction.

You will gain a whole new relationship with the Jewish people. You will find yourself criticizing their political viewpoints, praising their unity in defeating the Arabs, and randomly pointing them out whenever they appear on the television.

But you will also find yourself with a new warmth in your heart that never existed before. A warmth that exists for a homeland unrealized, a national potential waiting to be unleashed. You will realize that you start saying "Palestine" whenever possible. And if you have been truly and fully infected with the Palestinian bug, you will notice that whenever you hear the word, you will get butterflies in your stomach, just like the rest of us do.

White Americans are not the only victims, however. On my last trip to Palestine, I noticed Israelis smoking hookahs and saying "Yalla." Our aura is contagious. Israelis might try to pretend like we don't exist, but it's futile. We and our cultural awesomeness aren't going anywhere. Just ask Mark.

A little bit of Israel

August 13, 2011

"There's a little bit of Israel in all of us... Come find the Israel in you."

That's what I heard. I was up at 3 am. It was one of those nights when I couldn't sleep. I laid awake, working out varied scenarios and schemes to liberate my homeland. Then on came a commercial, showing stunning images of a familiar land, ending with the tagline:

There's a little bit of Israel in all of us... Come find the Israel in you.

As it turns out, about a year ago, Israel's Ministry of Tourism started an aggressive $10 million advertising campaign on American TV. It began in a few select cities, and has finally made its way to Detroit, the home of Arab America. I guess Detroit wasn't one of their initial target markets.

There's a little bit of Israel in all of us... Come find the Israel in you.

I can't get it out of my head. I have to admit, those guys are good at finding the right lines...

A land without a people for a people without a land.
Palestinians never miss an opportunity to miss an opportunity.
There's a little bit of Israel in all of us... Come find the Israel in you.

So I started to think. Is there a little bit of Israel in me? Well, my dad was born in March of 1948 and became a refugee at one month old. So, there's some Israel in him. My mom was born as an Israeli citizen. She and her family were eventually "diswelcomed" from their home in Akka by the Israeli government. There's definitely some Israel in her.

Palestinians spend our daily lives being completely consumed by being Palestinian. We live lives that are completely intertwined with Israel, whether we like it or not, and whether we live there or not. I spend the greater amount of my writ-

40

ing, speaking, and performing describing what it is like to be a Palestinian, an existence that relentlessly endeavors to endure in the face of constant Israeli attempts to deny it.

So, is there a little bit of Israel in me? No... There's A LOT! But, funny enough, I'm pretty sure the Ministry of Tourism wasn't referring to me in its commercials. The "Israel" that's in me isn't the "Israel" they're trying to sell. Their "Israel" is all about beautiful beaches. Mine is about uprooted olive trees. Their "Israel" is about hip art colonies. Mine is about the village they destroyed to house the artists. Their "Israel" is about great tasting hummus... Well, mine is too.

My Israel is about dispossession, disenfranchisement, and disavowal. My Israel is about an existence denied. My Israel is about generations of Palestinians circling the earth, able to live and succeed everywhere except where they belong. My Israel is about 10 refugee camps in Jordan, 12 in Lebanon, 10 in Syria, 19 in the West Bank, 8 in Gaza, and over 4.3 million registered Palestinian refugees. My Israel is about all the things Israel never wants to talk about. My Israel is about Palestine.

There's more than just a little bit of Israel in me. There's almost a hundred years worth.

Although it has not been covered in the American media at all, Israel has recently been the scene of mass demonstrations by Jews, protesting against living conditions that are becoming too costly to endure. The Israeli economy is suffering, in no small part due to the brutal occupation and ongoing building of illegal settlements that have diverted huge amounts of government money away from most of Israeli society.

In the wake of the Arab Spring and massive demonstrations throughout the Arab World by young citizens demanding accountability and change from their governments, Israelis are following suit.

There might be a little bit of Israel in all of us, but it looks like there is some of us in them too.

41

There is a place called Palestine

September 20, 2011

Sometime this week, Mahmoud Abbas will be asking the United Nations Security Council for full recognition for the State of Palestine. Such a move would give the Palestinians full rights at the UN, allowing them to vote, actively participate in the body's proceedings, and pursue legal action against Israel in international courts. The United States, as a permanent member of the Security Council, has voiced its intention to veto the proposal, basically rendering it dead on arrival.

This move at the UN also finally puts a nail in the coffin of the 1993 Oslo Accords, which we Palestinians all know was also dead on arrival, as we have witnessed 18 years of escalated settlement building, land confiscations, and flouting of international law.

Israel and America have been scurrying to spin the whole episode, as it is kind of making them look bad. It looks like we Palestinians might be finally winning a fight in the media. I knew we were doing OK when I saw Rick Perry and Mitt Romney expressing their (newly found) undying love for Israel all over the news this morning. Rick Perry, for those of you who might not know, is the frontrunner for the Republican presidential candidacy, as well as the current governor of Texas. He held a press conference today in New York City alongside prominent members of the Jewish lobby, where he dropped all the necessary taglines, like "moral equivalency," Jerusalem staying under complete Israeli control, and moving the US embassy from Tel Aviv to Jerusalem. He also said, "America should not be ambivalent between the terrorist tactics of Hamas and the security tactics of the legitimate and free state of Israel." Of course, any fully conscious observer of this whole affair would know that Hamas is against the push for UN recognition. So there, Rick Perry, you don't only agree with Israel, you agree with Hamas too! But I don't take Rick Perry for a very knowledgeable individual on Jews or Arabs... he's been trapped in Texas his whole life. I'm not sure he'd seen Jews anywhere other than TV before today. At the end of the press conference, I think I heard him lean over and say, "So when do I get to meet Jerry Seinfeld?"

42

As far I'm concerned, Israel can have Mitt Romney, Rick Perry, and their newest sweetheart, Sarah Palin. I'll take Barack Obama, even if he's kind of in the closet on the whole thing. President Obama, I thought we repealed "Don't Ask, Don't Tell"?

For a long time, I have been trying to keep alive a sort of Palestinian narrative, doing my best to remind Israel, America, and the rest of the world that we exist. We are now trying to get the UN to do that too, by finally recognizing that there is a place called "Palestine." The truth is that there has always been a place called "Palestine." I constantly hear supporters of Israel say that there is not, and never was, a place called "Palestine." It's not on the map, they say.

But I beg to differ.

There's no place called Palestine? Tell that to the 750 Palestinians in Arkansas. No, I don't mean the ones that own the gas stations and supermarkets. I mean the good football-loving people of Palestine, Arkansas. I heard once that Bill Clinton liked Palestinian women. Now it all makes sense.

No place called Palestine? There might be about 1400 people in Illinois who would disagree. No, I don't mean the brown Palestinians in Chicago. I'm talking about the good white people of Palestine, Illinois, the oldest incorporated village in the state. Take that for history!

Seriously, nowhere called Palestine? Maybe Rick Perry should watch his words, so as not to demean his 19,000 constituents in Palestine, Texas. This place called Palestine has a mayor, a college campus, and a high school that belongs to the "Palestine Independent School District." It's nice to see "Palestine" and "Independent" in the same name.

Do I have to keep going? OK, I will. There's a Palestine on the map in Ohio. That one only has 170 people living in it. It used to contain a lot more people until all of its residents were expelled in 1948 after… wait, I'm getting confused.

Indiana actually has two tiny little towns called Palestine with almost no people, and one much bigger one named New Palestine. The population of New Palestine, Indiana in the year 2000 was about 1200 people. Today, it's over 2100 people! In Indiana, the population of Palestinians is skyrocketing!

Palestinians are everywhere, and we are not going anywhere. I ask for solidarity from my fellow Palestinians in Arkansas, Illinois, Texas, Ohio, and Indiana. I have always supported their right to independence and self-determination. I am now asking for the same in return.

43

There is a place called Palestine. And whether it's a city in Texas, or a triangular piece of land on the Mediterranean Sea, there's nothing Netanyahu, Perry, and Obama can do or say to make it go away.

As it turns out, there is one town in America named Israel. It is located in the state of West Virginia, where there are also two towns called Palestine. I don't know if the Israelis in West Virginia were aware that there were Palestinians living in their state before they got there. But you can imagine my horror at seeing their city motto:

A farmland for a people for a people without a farmland.

A letter to Barack

November 23, 2011

Dear Barack,

We Arabs and Muslims in this country were so excited when you won in 2008. We all wanted to have you over for dinner. You like lamb, right?

During your inauguration, when Chief Justice John Roberts said "Barack HUSSEIN Obama," we loved it. We all started calling each other. "Did you hear him say 'Hussein'? That was awesome!"

We thought we were entering a new dawn of Arab and Muslim American life. Maybe we wouldn't get discriminated against as much anymore. Maybe relations with our homelands would get better. Maybe there will be an end to Islamophobia... Maybe, just maybe, there will finally be peace.

Remember when you said "Assalaamu Alaykum" in Cairo in 2009? I know you said it in an American accent to fool everyone back here. But we know you can do it right. It would be nice if every now and then you came out and said, "Look everyone, I know a lot of Muslims... I'm related to a lot of Muslims... I'm kinda Muslim... They're not that bad."

We thought it would just be a matter of time before you closed Guantanamo, or before you stopped racial profiling, or before we got a box on the census form. We hoped it wouldn't be too long before you put Israel in place, creating some sort of evenhandedness in Palestine.

Well, we were wrong.

Guantanamo is still there. Islam is still the enemy. And Israel is still running circles around human rights and international law. You have not been able to do any of the things we Arabs and Muslims elected you for! Having a Muslim president has not turned out the way we thought it would.

So Barack, we are angry with you. Now, we're not angry with you the same way the Tea Party people are. We don't hate you. We don't want your demise. We don't think it's a good idea to hold up signs of you dressed like an African chief with a horn through your nose. We're mad at you the same way we get angry with someone in our family. We're disappointed. Our feelings are hurt.

45

We remember when you said, "The United States does not accept the legitimacy of continued Israeli settlements." We loved that. We remember when you said, "it also undeniable that the Palestinian people - Muslims and Christians - have suffered in pursuit of a homeland." That was awesome. We were pinching ourselves. But those words seem like an eternity ago now.

Now you tell us that Jerusalem will never be divided, that it will be the eternal capital of Israel. You tell us that we have no place in the UN. You tell us that we don't belong in the international community, or that our aspirations are not good enough, or that we can't have a voice. We're pissed.

Barack, you need to give a little back to the Arab and Muslim community, because, frankly, we've let you get away with a lot. And it's all because you're "kinda Muslim." For instance, if you were a Bible-thumping president from Texas, we would have booed you when you came to Cairo two years ago. But since you're a "kinda Muslim" president from Kenya, we cheered and cheered. If your name was Mitt, Newt, Herman, Rick, or Jon, we would have thought it was very suspicious when you helped in Egypt, dropped bombs in Libya, and called for the ouster of (almost) every Arab dictator. But your name is Barack and you're "kinda Muslim," so it was cool. And, finally, if you were pasty white and clearly NOT Muslim, people would have demonstrated in the streets throughout the Arab and Muslim world when you secretly assassinated Osama bin Laden and Anwar al-Awlaki (an American citizen, by the way). But you're black and "kinda Muslim," so they let it go.

Look, we know you have it tough. Being the first (and maybe last) black president must weigh heavily on you. We know there's still racism in America. Trust me, we know. People think that everything is OK because we Americans elected a black man to become president. You proved that a black man could get elected president if he went to Harvard Law School, was a law professor, has written a few books, is only really half black, isn't named Tyrone, was born in Hawaii and not Detroit, and is one of the most eloquent and moving speakers we've ever seen. George W. Bush proved that any white guy could be president.

So, Barack, habibi, cousin, come back home. There's a warm seat for you at the dinner table. The lamb is in the fridge.

Shafeeq, the hummus-lover

December 2, 2011

Shafeeq Zahr was born in Nazareth around 1912. He was smart, funny, and dashingly good-looking. He was a Palestinian, and he loved hummus.

His mother died of complications during his birth, and his father quickly remarried. After his teenage years, Shafeeq left Nazareth and eventually settled in the beautiful Palestinian seaside city of Yafa. At that time, Yafa was the economic, political, and cultural center of Palestine. He became a Christian missionary, worked as a construction worker, and was from then on known by his baptismal name of Elias (Arabic for Elijah).

In the early 1940s, after performing work on her family's house, Elias met Salma Manoli. Salma was a teacher in Yafa, and they soon decided to be married. Before they were married, however, Shafeeq, in hopes of bettering his life, and perhaps to fall into good graces, volunteered to fight for the colonial British in World War II. Of course, the British at that time controlled Palestine. Elias performed his duties for the British during the war, where he was captured by and eventually escaped from German forces. He returned from the war, with many physical scars, and returned to Yafa, where he finally married Salma. In March 1948, George, their first child, was born. George, a Palestinian, loves hummus too... with lots of olive oil.

One month later, Zionist forces (with the support of the British government) took Yafa by military force, forcing tens of thousands of Arabs from the city, including Elias, Salma, and their infant child. After fighting and risking his life for the British government, he returned to his homeland only to find that the same government that he had fought for had "given" it to a foreign people. I think I know how Elias must have felt. One time I took a girl out, bought her an expensive dinner, and even got a flat tire on the way home. I didn't care though, because we had a great time, and we even planned to see each other again. We had a real connection. The next night, I saw her out with another guy, not nearly as smart or handsome. When I went over to say hello, she said looked me

47

up and down and said, "Who are you again?" I was so depressed... I drove on that flat tire for a month.

Elias refuged to Amman, continued to feast on hummus, and eventually put down roots in a poor neighborhood named Jabal al-Hashimiyeh a-Shamaliyeh. Using his skills in construction, he bought some used crates and built a small wooden structure for his young family. He worked mainly as a carpenter in Amman, and Elias and Salma lived the life of refugees, earning meager wages and surviving on monthly UN rations of flour, sugar, milk, and beans.

In Nazareth, Musa, Elias' father, knew nothing of his son. He had assumed that Elias had died in World War II. By 1960, Elias' neighborhood in Amman had grown, and a small church had been built. The parish priest there, also a native of Nazareth, knew Elias and Salma well. As a religious official, that priest traveled freely between Jordan and Israel. During a trip in 1960, he noticed something peculiar in a Nazareth church: a memorial dedicated in the name of a lost loved one... Elias Zahr.

The priest quickly found Musa, the father of this memorialized man, telling him something unbelievable: "I think I know your son... and he is in Amman." In order to prove that Elias was who they thought he might be, the church asked Musa to formulate a set of questions to be sent to Amman, questions that only Musa's true son could answer. Elias passed the test with flying colors. As an Arab-Israeli Christian, Musa was permitted to enter the old city of Jerusalem (at that time part of Jordan) once a year for religious purposes. He arranged to meet his son there. Elias, Salma, and their young son George traveled from Amman to Jerusalem for the occasion. Father and son were briefly reunited, but 24 hours later, Musa had to return to Israel. Similar visits occurred over the next few years.

In early 1967, after a dispute with his own family, Musa angrily left Nazareth. I can just imagine him exclaiming, "Fine, I will go live with my son in Amman!" He illegally crossed into the northern West Bank, but he was an old man. He did not make it far before he was captured by Jordanian forces, who thought at first he might be some sort of smuggler, or worse yet, a spy. He was detained for a few weeks and sent back to Nazareth. He might be the only Palestinian ever actually deported back to Israel.

Elias and Musa never met again.

Elias continued his hard life in Amman. Although Palestinians were granted citizenship in Jordan, they were and remain second-class citizens. King Hussein constantly cracked down on them, most notably during the fighting of the fall of 1970, dubbed "Black September." During that time, the Jordanian army killed at least 10,000 Palestinians. Elias and his family sought shelter under their one-room house.

George graduated from college in Jordan, went to study further in Beirut, and eventually earned a PhD from the University of California-Berkeley, where he married a fellow Palestinian refugee. In 1977, he returned to Amman and became a professor at the University of Jordan. In 1979, as a result of an ugly and unjust political episode, George, wildly popular with his students, was fired from his post. He was exiled from Jordan and found a new life in America. Elias, like Musa, had lost his son.

Later in 1979, Elias died in his sleep in Amman. It is said that he died from a heart attack. But it could have been that he had simply had enough. George could not return to Jordan for his father's funeral, knowing he would face certain arrest.

Elias was my grandfather. His legacy lives through George (my father) and me (and my siblings). Of course, we both share his intelligence, humor, and handsome looks. We also carry on his Palestinian story. Yes, we enjoy life and we laugh like everyone else. But we always have that little hole in our hearts. As human beings, we are thankful for what we have... As Palestinians, we are always aware of what we don't.

Things, however, are changing. The world can try to reject our past, but it can't deny our future. I happen to think my future is bright... and it's full of Palestinian hummus.

Now we're invented?

So I was watching the news on Friday (as I always do... remember, CNN is a social activity for Palestinians), and I heard Newt Gingrich say the following:

> *Newt on CNN: I believe that the Jewish people have the right to have a state.*
> *Me at home: OK...*
> *Newt on CNN: Remember, there was no Palestine as a state. It was part of the Ottoman Empire.*
> *Me at home: Uh oh.*
> *Newt on CNN: And I think we've had an invented Palestinian people, who are in fact Arabs, who are historically part of the Arab community.*
> *Me at home: Huh?*

Now, as a Palestinian, I've heard a lot of racist stuff about us. I've heard Abba Eban say that Palestinians "never miss an opportunity to miss an opportunity." I've heard Menachem Begin call us "beasts" and Ehud Barak call us "crocodiles." I've even heard Ariel Sharon say he would "kill as many Arabs as necessary."

But now, we're "invented?" I'm still not sure what it means. So, were we there before Israel? Were we not there? Lies about us usually have some level of clarity. But this one is just confusing. I want to be mad. I do. But I just don't know how to feel.

Now, to be fair, Newt does have some company. Golda Meir was the Prime Minister of Israel from 1969-1974 and she said a lot of stuff about us. Most famously, she told the world, "There is no such thing as a Palestinian people... It is not as if we came and threw them out and took their country. They didn't exist." When addressing the Palestinian right of return to their homeland, she stated, "We shall not let this happen." She defiantly told us, "Arab sovereignty in Jerusalem just cannot be." And to top it all off, she declared, "How can we return the occupied territories? There is no one to return them to."

So I guess Newt Gingrich can claim some sort of camaraderie with Golda Meir. But that's nothing to be proud of. She was more evil than Ann Coulter, Casey Anthony, Lady Macbeth, and Meryl Streep in "The Devil Wears Prada"... combined.

Of course, Newt was just trying to cozy up to Jewish voters in America by telling them something he believed they wanted to hear. But doesn't he know that denying our existence is out of style? Even the Israelis now acknowledge our existence. Benjamin Netanyahu calls us a "demographic threat." See Newt, you can't be a threat if you don't exist!

But being "invented" might not be that bad. People have invented things that were really beneficial, like penicillin, the smoke detector, and seatbelts. A lot of really cool stuff was invented too, like the Internet, the iPhone, and Twinkies. But I listened to Newt's tone when he spoke. Somehow I don't think he meant we were a "good" invention. My suspicion is that he was lumping us in with the bad inventions, like the Snuggie, the Macarena, and Farmville. I think he meant the world "invented" the Palestinians, just like it "invented," say, Kim Kardashian.

In last night's Republican debate, Newt staunchly defended his comments, saying that what he said was "factually accurate." But he didn't stop there. He said Palestinians were "terrorists," and that we have hateful entries in our textbooks like, "if there are 13 Jews and 9 Jews are killed, how many Jews are left?" The claim that that sort of stuff is in Palestinian textbooks is, of course, false and racist. But in case he was wondering, the answer is 4. We're not a bunch of inhumane savages, but we're not dumb either.

At any rate, we Palestinians have been around for a very long time. Just ask Jesus. But all this talk about inventions does remind me of another famous Israeli quote spoken by David Ben-Gurion, the chief "inventor" of Israel:

Jewish villages were built in the place of Arab villages. You do not even know the names of these Arab villages, and I do not blame you because geography books no longer exist. Not only do the books not exist, the Arab villages are not there either. Nahlal arose in the place of Mahlul, Kibbutz Gvat in the place of Jibta, Kibbutz Sarid in the place of Huneifis, and Kefar Yehushua in the place of Tal al-Shuman. There is not a single place built in this country that did not have a former Arab population.

51

We are not "invented." But our struggle was... by the same people that deny it today.

Happy birthday Jesus... you're one of us!

December 27, 2011

Well, another Christmas has come and gone. To Palestinians, this holiday is really special. Jesus was one of us. We're pretty proud of that. I've been to Bethlehem, Nazareth, and Jerusalem many times, and Palestinians are looking after Jesus' stuff pretty well.

Now, for me, Christmas is really cool. As I've mentioned before, both of my parents are Palestinian. My father is Christian, and my mother is Muslim. To some, this union might seem like it would produce some bizarre results. It's important to note, though, that all four of my parents' children are great successes. There's a high school math teacher working at a prestigious school in Jordan, a management consultant working for a prestigious firm in Dubai, a music manager working for a prestigious artist in New York City, and me: a college student who started as a chemistry major, then received a degree in history, then a master's degree in Middle East studies, then a law degree, and then became, logically, a comedian. See, I'm not confused at all.

Growing up in my house was fun. We celebrated everything: Eid, Easter, Eid, and Christmas. One year we even celebrated Yom Kippur for good measure. We moved to America when I was only three years old. A few years later, my grandmother moved here too. And she lived with us. Arab mother in laws are notoriously difficult. They're especially cranky when their Christian son marries a Muslim girl. My grandmother came to this country because both of her children had moved here and my grandfather had passed away. Unlike some others, we Arabs don't leave our old people alone, and we don't put them in retirement homes. They live with us until we hang their portrait on the wall.

I remember when my grandmother moved into our house, because she didn't come alone. She brought with her something extremely special. She brought with her a memento of another famous Palestinian ... a beautiful, huge portrait of the Virgin Mary. That portrait stayed in our house until she passed away in 2005. While I've been visiting my parents for this holiday, I have asked where that portrait was. Only one person knows: my mom. That's right, my Muslim mom has been protecting that portrait of the Virgin Mary all this time. She won't tell anyone where it is. That's how seriously she's protecting it. She won't tell anyone... anyone.

My childhood was happy and fun. And no time was ever more fun than Christmas. My grandmother especially loved it. She would get us lavish gifts, like homemade sweaters, striped socks, and collared shirts. Hey, she lived most of her adult life surviving on food rations and donated clothes. To her, new clothes were like a new Ferrari. Actually, she had no idea what a Ferrari was.

My mom loved Christmas too. She decorated the tree, cooked a great dinner, and made sure we got at least a couple of the things on our Christmas list. My mom might be Muslim, but she definitely gets into the Christmas spirit.

Christmas for a Palestinian is bittersweet. People around the world are celebrating something that happened in the place we call home. And they visit Palestine to see things that we are proud to protect. Remembering Jesus and Mary tells us once again that our history is deep, expansive, and proud. It didn't start in the year 1948. It started before the years even had names.

But while Christmas allows us Palestinians to dwell on our treasured history, it is also a present reminder of where we are today. Like Jesus, we have been told that we do not belong in Palestine. Like us, he was told that his stories have no place there. Like him, we have been driven out. Like us, he fought against power. Like him, we refuse to shut up.

Jesus is revered in both Christianity and Islam. As my saying goes, "Muslims are nice, they love Jesus Christ." His tradition is protected by all of us, Muslims and Christians alike. We Palestinians have always stayed linked by our common stories and experiences. Since Jesus is one of us, Muslims and Christians among us have always gotten along in his backyard. My house just happens to be a place where they actually sleep in the same bed.

Jesus once said, "That which you do to the least of my brethren, you do to me." Those words hold especially true for Palestinians, as rockets, bulldozers, and prime ministers don't care whether or not their victims eat pork. They want to do away with us either way.

Now, I'm not too religious, but I love celebrating this particular Palestinian's birthday every December 25. I particularly love remembering the truest parallel between him and us, his brethren 2000 years later. Like him, we spend our days telling our stories to anyone who will listen. We're protecting everything that belonged to Jesus, including the truth.

Me, a victim of anti-Semitism...

December 31, 2011

This week, I experienced a kind of confusing racism I never could have imagined. Since I am proud of my heritage, I celebrate Christmas because it is the birthday of the most famous Palestinian of all time. In the spirit of the season, I bought each of my two sisters a Tommy Hilfiger bag from the well-known discount store Marshall's. Yes, I shop at Marshall's. I'm an Arab Palestinian and I've been culturally indoctrinated to never pay full price for anything.

On Christmas morning, I presented my sisters with their gifts. They didn't care for them too much. So they told me, "Thanks for the gesture, but just return them and get your money back." I asked my mom if she knew anyone who might want the bags. She thought about it and couldn't come up with any takers. I happened to think the bags were very cute.

So I went to get my money back. As I pulled up, I searched for my receipt. Damn, I had lost it. I entered Marshall's, receipt-less, with the two beautiful, trendy bags I had bought. The manager was a nice 20-something white woman who couldn't have been kinder. She explained to me that without a receipt, I could only receive a store credit, in the form of a gift card. This was no problem. I would give the card to my father. He would appreciate my gift. He's a true bargain hunter, and he shops at Marshall's almost daily. Where do you think I got it from?

As the manager worked through my transaction, I noticed a rack of gift cards on the counter with a few different designs. I asked her if I could have one of those nice-looking gift cards. She very politely obliged. One card in particular caught my eye. It was blue, contained the Marshall's logo, and had written upon it a delightful holiday message: "Happy Hanukkah."

I thought this was great. I would get my dad the "Happy Hanukkah" gift card. I thought it would be hilarious for a man who was kicked out of Palestine, grew up in refugee camps, and lived on UN rations to walk around with a "Happy Hanukkah" gift card. As a comedian, I was basically required to take advantage of this opportunity. My dad is a staunch lover of Palestine, but even he wouldn't turn down a

$60 Marshall's gift card, no matter what was inscribed upon it.

I pulled the "Happy Hanukkah" gift card from the display and handed it to the pleasant young lady. Now, I should give a little note about where I grew up. I was raised in an area just outside of Philadelphia almost completely inhabited by very nice white people. I mean it was our family, an Indian family, a black family, and the rest were all white people. And we almost never had any problems. They loved us. They even elected my dad to the public school board. And this Marshall's manager was one of these very nice people.

I handed her the "Happy Hanukkah" gift card. She looked at the card, looked at me, looked at the card again, and looked at me again. Then she said, "You know this says 'Hanukkah,' right?" I paused, and said, "Yes, I know that." She smiled, completed the transaction, gave me the card, and I walked out.

As I started to drive away, I thought, "Wait a second! That was messed up! What if I were a Jew? I would've been really offended! How dare she say that?" Then I realized something much bigger. I had just experienced real life anti-Semitism! I was a victim of rampant, ugly, disgusting anti-Semitism. This was horrible. I've experienced and seen lots of racism. But I've only read about anti-Semitism in history books, Wikipedia, and Palestinian textbooks.

But I was also thrilled to so glaringly discover that we Jews and Arabs share something very special. As it turns out, white people don't like either of us. I always thought Jews were exaggerating about anti-Semitism. Boy, was I wrong.

I am not a Jew, but at that moment I felt the weight of thousands of years of persecution, discrimination, and oppression. I now know what it is like, in some small way, to be a Jew. Now, if only I could get through Israeli security with just a smile, I would be all set. I think I've earned my entry into the club. After all, I'm probably the first-ever Palestinian victim of anti-Semitism.

I mean, technically, we're both Semites anyway. We both have big noses and neurotic moms. We're both hairy and hate paying full price. The only real difference is that Jews are chosen by God, and we're usually chosen by airport security.

I finally got home and gave my dad his gift card. He laughed. I get my sense of humor from him too. I also described my traumatic experience to him. I told him, "Can you believe she said that?" He replied, "Well, maybe she said that because Hanukkah is over." I was shocked again. My dad

57

knows when Hanukkah ends? I don't even know when it starts. I know it's eight days long, but that's only because I heard it in an Adam Sandler song. If I were a Jew, I clearly wouldn't be a very good one.

As I thought about it, maybe he was right. I should give that Marshall's manager the benefit of the doubt. After all, I could have been the first Jew she had ever encountered.

Cosby, MacGyver, & the news

January 21, 2012

I've always been prone to lose things. It's probably because
I enjoyed a fairly privileged upbringing. I grew up middle-
class and fortunately never really wanted for anything. My
siblings and I didn't grow up overly spoiled, but we had all
that we needed and more. Sure, it took a long time to get my
dad to buy us a Nintendo, but I think that's because he believed that a TV alone was luxury enough.

My dad grew up on UN rations, living hand to mouth. As a
Palestinian refugee, he had nothing in the way of luxury.
Now, after long struggles, he has settled into an upper mid-
dle-class American lifestyle, and he always has taken very
close care of his possessions. It's not too surprising. He grew
up with nothing, so he always knows where all his stuff is. He
keeps everything organized and doesn't take his precious effects for granted as his children sometimes do. In fact, he
couldn't understand how I could lose anything when I was a
kid. I remember what he used to say:

Me: Baba, I lost my toy truck.
Him: Well, where was the last place you left it?
Me: In my room.
Him: So it used to be there right?
Me: Yeah.
Him: And now it's just gone?
Me: Ummm... Yeah.
Him: Well, I guess we should call the news then.
Me: Huh?
Him: "Yes, we should call the news... I think they would be
very interested to know that a toy truck can just get up and
walk away."

I think I might have gotten my sarcasm from him.
My dad definitely encouraged us to appreciate what we
had. And he taught us to take responsibility for both our actions and our possessions. But this routine of his sometimes
made it hard to talk to him. It was difficult to share some of
my struggles with him:

59

Me: Baba, my girlfriend just dumped me.
Him: But she used to be there right?
Me: Yeah.
Him: And now she's just gone?
Me: Yeah.
Him: Well, I guess we should call the news then.

We Palestinians watch the news so much that we think we actually know the anchors. I was probably the only kid in the fourth grade who actually knew who Tom Brokaw and Dan Rather were. Other kids might have called Superman if they needed help. I was supposed to call Peter Jennings.

But we didn't only watch the news. My dad let us watch a couple other shows too. On Thursday nights, we all got together and watched "The Cosby Show." My dad loved that show. We Palestinians identify closely with blacks and their struggle. Like they once did, we are now fighting for recognition in the face of a structure built to defeat us and silence our narrative. I actually almost checked "African-American" on the census form last year. We Arabs are, indeed, very similar to black people. We get profiled. We get blamed for stuff we don't do. And white people cross the street when they see us coming. Also, like black people, we have Sunday dinners and large families. Our families are so large that an Arab is sometimes older than his uncle. You know you're an Arab if you've ever taken your uncle to Chuck E. Cheese. Finally, our cuisines share a lot in common. Go to an Arab barbeque and you'll see it... There are watermelons everywhere!

The other show my dad always watched with us was "MacGyver." MacGyver could make anything out of anything. My dad used to say he was our cousin, though I've never seen him at any family functions. My dad was just as resourceful as MacGyver was. I'm sure that came from his tough upbringing. My father can make a pair of shoes with four rubber bands and two pieces of cardboard. Now that I think back about it, there was one thing MacGyver made in almost every episode: a bomb. He was blowing stuff up all the time. If he was my cousin, I hope CNN doesn't find out.

I have kept the lessons I learned from watching TV with my dad. He, like most Palestinian parents, instilled in his children a deep appreciation of our past and an acute desire to announce and defend the justice inherent in our struggle. We were taught to be proud of who we were, just like the Cosbys. And now as an adult, I have my own house, and I'm renovating the whole thing. I'm being inventive and enterprising as I move along, and I'm doing my best to creatively solve the problems I encounter, just like MacGyver.

My father's lessons have proved useful to me, like during the last time I was questioned at Tel Aviv's airport after hours of waiting:

Israeli soldier: How long will you be staying in Israel?
Me: You know what? I'm not going to Israel...
I'm going to Palestine!
Soldier: There is no Palestine.
Me: Yes there is!
Soldier (pointing to a map on the wall): Look, there is no Palestine on the map!
Me: Wow... But it used to be there right?
Soldier: Yeah.
Me: And now it's just gone?
Soldier: Yeah.
Me: Well, I guess we should call the news then.

I love my mom

February 4, 2012

We don't get to choose our moms, so I consider myself pretty lucky. She has been unconditionally loving and supportive. Most moms are like that. She has been proud when I have done well. Most moms are like that too. And she has let me know when I have messed up. I think just about every mom is like that.

But my mom is different.

My mom always made sure we did our homework. She let us know that "good enough" would never be good enough. Today, three of her four children are independent, dynamic individuals who command and give great respect. And I'm a law school graduate who became a comedian. Three out of four isn't bad. She's pretty awesome.

I love my mom because she taught me how to appreciate food. She didn't boil hot dogs for dinner. When my mom complained that she was slaving all day in the kitchen, it was because she was actually slaving all day in the kitchen. And we ate like kings every night. She always made everything from scratch. Hamburger Helper was not welcome in our home. I think the list of things never allowed in our house went something like Ariel Sharon's picture, the Israeli flag, and Hamburger Helper. Her cooking has become the stuff of legend in the Philadelphia Arab-American community. Sure, every now and then she took a little break and made us something a little less laborious, like spaghetti, with homemade meatballs, and for some reason, chick peas.

I love my mom because she taught me how to be resourceful. We always had more grocery bags than the rest of the neighborhood combined. White people throw away their bags. We didn't. Ours were stuffed in that little space between the refrigerator and the wall. White moms asked their kids if they wanted turkey or roast beef for lunch. My mom asked me if I wanted paper or plastic.

In 1965, at the age of 11, my mother came to America from Palestine with her parents and three sisters. Her father ventured here with the intention of studying and returning to a job in Israel. My mom got here by taking a boat from Haifa to

New York, then a bus from New York to California. That was a long trip. She survived. I love her.

Due to some horrible (but typical) actions by the Israel government, my grandfather was stripped of his job back in Israel and forced to stay in America to sustain a livelihood for his wife and four daughters. Of course, being forced to stay in America is not that bad. I guess I'm glad he didn't decide to study in Russia. But, of course, America wasn't home. I'm sure it was hard to adjust. As a teenage girl in California in the sixties, my mom must have gone through lots of growing pains. She didn't freak out. I love her.

My mom fell in love with my dad while they were students at the same university. He was Christian. She was Muslim. She knew that marrying him would not be an easy thing to do. But she saw a proud Palestinian man, and not simply a man of a faith different than hers. She had the courage and strength to marry my dad despite the odds. Only when I got a little older did I understand what that truly meant. I really love her.

She made me into the Palestinian I am today. Every now and then she would wake us up early on a Saturday morning, stuff us in the car, and take us somewhere fun like New York or Washington DC. When we arrived at our destination, sometimes to our surprise, we would be in the middle of a demonstration. Being Palestinian is only partly genetic. You get the important stuff when your mom tells you about it over and over and over again. And if there's anything Arab moms are good at, it's saying something over and over and over again.

I love my mom because she showed me what it means to be generous and gracious. My parents have always been very active in the community, and have always been overly giving and kind. The long line of Arab and Arab-American students who have come to study in Philadelphia and found a second home with the Zahrs could attest to this fact.

Today is my mom's birthday. Yes, my mom. My loving, supportive, demanding, hard-working, resourceful, determined, strong, generous, gracious, and courageous mom. My Palestinian mom! I have tried to learn from her example. Mom, I'm doing my best.

House hunting in Jerusalem

February 10, 2012

I love watching reality TV. Whether it's "Cupcake Wars," "Storage Wars," or "Shipping Wars," I just can't get enough. And no, I don't just like watching them because I'm an Arab and they all have the word "war" in the title.

A particular favorite of mine is "House Hunters." In this show, the cameras follow an individual, couple, or family searching for a new home. As a Palestinian, I am familiar with this concept. We have been searching for 64 years.

Anyway, each show features three properties, and at the end of the broadcast, the buyer chooses one as his new residence. The show is extremely popular and has produced an interesting spinoff, "House Hunters International." In this version, the buyer looks to buy a home in a different country than his or her current country of residence. A few nights ago, I happened to be watching when a very interesting episode aired: "House Hunters International: Jerusalem." A very nice Orthodox Jewish woman named Hayley was looking to relocate from New Jersey to Israel. She wanted her children to have the experience of growing up in the Holy Land.

Hayley arrived in Israel to look at three houses. I imagine she had an easier time getting through Tel Aviv airport security than I do. She made her way to Jerusalem and began her search.

The first house Hayley looked at was in the "fashionable neighborhood of Baka." A quick fact here. Wealthy Muslim and Christian Palestinian families established Baka in the 1920's. After 1948, Baka ended up in West Jerusalem, inside Israel. As a result of this development, in Baka, "the population changed." (Wikipedia) "Changed" is a nice way of putting it. In reality, the Arab families who built those houses were expelled.

The second and third homes Hayley looked at were located in the German Colony, what the narrator referred to as a "pre-war neighborhood." Before 1948, affluent Arab families who had built mansions there called it home. After 1948, "the abandoned homes were used to house new immigrants." (Thanks again Wikipedia) "Abandoned" is a nice way of putting it. In reality, the German Colony was ethnically cleansed of its Arab population.

All three houses were brimming with Arab architecture. As Hayley walked through the homes, I heard things like:

She wants a traditional, old Jerusalem home.
This house was built in the 1920's.
It's got the tiles, built in the old style.
The arches... love it!
This is authentic.

For those of you don't speak "Israeli," let me translate:

Traditional, old = Palestinian
Built in the 1920's = Palestinian
Tiles in the old style = Palestinian
Arches = Palestinian
Authentic = Palestinian

I guess that even though Israelis definitely don't want us there, they really like our style. And I don't blame them. We Palestinians are pretty cool. They even made falafel and hummus part of Israeli national cuisine. It's not that surprising actually. When you can steal someone's home without thinking twice, swiping the recipes too is really easy.

After the 1967 war, Israel "united" East and West Jerusalem. The Palestinian residents who remain hold Jerusalem ID cards. They are "permanent residents" of Israel, pay Israeli taxes, are citizens of no country, and do not vote in national elections. We have "permanent residents" here in America, but they came from Mexico. The "permanent residents" of Jerusalem came from Jerusalem. They must periodically renew their status, and if they are absent for more than seven years, they forever lose their "right" of residency. Of course, Jews can become full citizens of Israel whenever they like. And they can buy abandoned homes with authentic tiles and arches.

Israel looks to rid herself of all Palestinian presence, and nowhere is this more evident than in Jerusalem. All Israeli politicians repetitively proclaim that Jerusalem will remain the "eternal and undivided capital of Israel." Simply put, it is Israel's view that the city cannot be Arab in any capacity. She would prefer we were never there. But the authentic tiles in Baka don't lie. They tell the world that Palestinians walked atop them. The stones of the walls don't lie either. They tell the world that they were painstakingly placed by Palestinians

65

who called Jerusalem home. And the arches don't lie. They tell the new residents, as they peer out onto the Old City, that no amount of denial can erase the Palestinians who perfected their symmetry.

As that episode came to a close, another one immediately followed. Apparently, I had stumbled onto a "House Hunters: International" marathon. Again, an Orthodox Jewish American couple was looking to relocate to a new country. This time, they were searching for a house in Costa Rica. Before I turned off the TV, I wished them the best of luck.

They tried to make her go to rehab, she said "No, no, no!"

March 11, 2012

I'm a Palestinian, so I watch the news all the time. And I've been intensely watching for the past week. And it's been ridiculous.

Benjamin Netanyahu visited Washington, DC and had a sit-down with President Barack Obama. They seemed happy to see each other... sort of. Netanyahu came into town to address the American Israel Public Affairs Committee (AIPAC), the largest and most influential American pro-Israel lobby group. Obama addressed them too, assuring everyone that he "has Israel's back."

The main issue was Iran, and nothing else. It was all Iran, all the time.

Obama has announced that he will try diplomacy first, and only bomb if he has to. Israel has announced that it will bomb first, and only try diplomacy if it has to. Israel is treating this whole Iran thing the same way an Arab mother sets up her son with a wife: Shoot first, ask questions later.

And I must say something here. I have watched American presidents and politicians for a long time. I have always accepted that they are beholden to the Israeli lobby. But, I have never seen them this subservient, this obedient, this meek. Yes, it is an election year, and everyone is being especially responsive to special interest groups. But this has been ridiculous.

Barack Obama has been particularly doting in his words, even expressing at times his disbelief that supporters of Israel would question his commitment to the Jewish State. Really, Barack? You're a black Harvard-trained civil-rights lawyer, so you can understand racism, recognize it, and eloquently fight against it. You've had Palestinian friends (despite your denials), so you might have heard our pitch a few times. Oh, and you're Muslim. News flash, Mr. President, Israel doesn't trust you.

Israel will probably attack Iran, but it will have very little to do with any sort of nuclear program that Iran is building. Israel needs war. She has an addiction, and war is the drug.

67

And she is a functioning addict. War makes her get up in the morning. War makes her look forward to the day. War gets her high.

Like any addict, she is in massive denial. She believes that there is no problem. She is arrogant, rude, impolite, vulgar, uncouth, discourteous, foul, offensive, and ill mannered (The "Thesaurus" function on Microsoft Word is really useful). She denies she is doing anything destructive. But as we all know, the addict does not go through her disease alone. Those closest to Israel are caught in her web as well. The denial of Palestinian history, rights, and simple humanity are not evidence of Israel's evil, just symptoms of her sickness. She is not a bad person. She just needs help.

America is, of course, Israel's enabler and dealer, feeding her addiction with unconditional support, constant coddling, and an endless amount of ammunition and protection. She needs her fix, and America helps make it possible. America's funding and political submission are just what Israel needs to get high. AIPAC gets in on the act too, coming up with any and all excuses to exempt her from any responsibility.

During Israel's visit, we Palestinians were nowhere in the discourse. Not a word. We were totally left out. That was fine with me. It seemed like we might be left alone for a little bit while Netanyahu dealt with Iran. No such luck. Immediately upon his return, he began a bombing campaign in Gaza that has killed almost 20 Palestinians in three days. He couldn't help himself. When a true addict sees even the smallest opportunity, he is powerless to fight the urge. That's how it works. A compulsive gambler should never have cash, and Netanyahu should never have Apache helicopters.

Israel's addiction has taken her through ups and downs, including one mild overdose (Lebanon 2006), and a few binges (Gaza 2009). Like any addict, she will eventually experience a major overdose (perhaps Iran). And when she overdoses, she will be left with the only two choices an addict in that position has. She will either die, or her friends will get together, have an intervention, and push her into rehab. The world has been trying to push Israel into therapy and counseling for some time, but her main enablers and dealers have continued to give her the illusion that she can handle her compulsive sickness, causing her to act more and more absurdly as time passes by. When Israel finally does enter rehab, her formula for recovery will be simple: a complete reversal of her current approach to life.

When that happens, I'll be the first one to hold her hand.

68

Israel's text messages revealed!

March 28, 2012

I'm not saying Israel has anything to hide, but this doesn't look good.

In the past few days, Israel has cut off all contact with the United Nations Human Rights Council. This move came after the UNHRC voted to send a fact-finding mission to the West Bank and East Jerusalem to assess the effects of Israeli settlements on everyday Palestinian life. Israel has said she will prevent the UNHCR team from entering the country to conduct their work.

Have you ever tried to look through your significant other's cell phone? Well, the UN wants to look through Israel's text messages, and Israel doesn't like it. She's freaking out. But it looks like 64 years of lying and cheating might be catching up to her.

Everything is crumbling around Israel. Her secrets are being exposed. In an amazing stroke of investigative journalism, I've gotten my hands on some of Israel's text messages, and they are revealing:

To Yasser Arafat (yes, Israel had text messaging way back in 1993):

hey, thx for signing that oslo thing... listen, we're going to keep building settlements if it's ok with you... i'm sure no one will ever say anything... anyway, looking fwd to the nobel peace prize ceremony... can you believe we're getting that! LMFAO!

To Jordan's King Abdullah:

looks like you're my only buddy around here... i'm coming to amman this weekend to relax... let's chill... hookah time!

To Husni Mubarak:

hey, the offer is still open... anytime u wanna come to tel aviv to retire, just lemme know... ur still my favorite muslim president :)

To Mahmud Ahmadinejad:

69

dude, we are so gonna bomb you!

To Muammar Qaddafi:

Why aren't you returning my msgs? miss u... u were my favorite muslim president... :(

To Bashar Al-Assad:

hey man, can you plz stop letting in observers and stuff? and i heard you just agreed to that un plan from kofi... OMG! i thought we had an agreement... you're kinda making me look like an a-hole. :/

To Barack Obama:

who's my president? you my president! you're voting no on the UN thing, right? duh, of course you are! i know you don't like the sound of 'one-term barack'... oh, and happy early ramadan! LOL! :P

To Newt Gingrich:

i just texted obama 'happy ramadan.' epic... anyway, gotta go and arrest some 'invented' people... xoxoxoxo.

To Barack Obama (the next day):

hey barack, listen, sorry about the whole 'happy ramadan' thing... i drank so much last night... i was building settlements all day... anyway, for real, do u mind voting no on that human rights council stuff? it kinda looks like everyone is voting against us. thx for ur help... ur my favorite muslim president ;)

To Benjamin Netanyahu (after the UNHCR vote):

you know what? F%^& THE UN... first the unesco thing, now this... hello?!?!? don't they know we're never giving back the west bank and east jerusalem!? keep building settlements... build, baby, build... btw, don't show this msg to anyone.

To Jon Stewart:

yo, i watch the daily show every day... ur kinda being a jerk.

To Amer Zahr:

70

yo, i read the civil arab all the time... ur definitely being a jerk.

To Steven Spielberg:

things are not looking very good... we need to make schindler's list 2 ASAP!

Indeed, things are not looking good for Israel, especially since Syria has agreed to a UN-based initiative and Iran has agreed to permit UN inspectors into its largest nuclear facility.

But I want to help, so I just sent Israel a text:

hey sweetie, how is my mom's hummus recipe treating you? anyway, i see things aren't going great for you... i think if we get on tv and hug, it might help... but you gotta stop stealing my land... anyway, call me, i'm free anytime... well, i'm not really 'free' LOL.

60 minutes of truth

April 28, 2012

A weird thing happened last week. A major American media outlet told the truth about the Israeli occupation of the West Bank. This, of course, upset many supporters of Israel. Nothing annoys Israel more than the truth.

On April 22, "60 Minutes" ran an in-depth piece on the plight of Palestinian Christians, pointing out that Christians have been leaving Palestine in startling numbers. Israel has consistently said that this is because of Islamic radicalism. The Palestinian Christians in the piece told a bit of a different story. They told the world they were suffering, and sometimes emigrating, for the same reason as any other Palestinian: the brutality of the Israeli occupation. A very famous Palestinian once said, "That which you do to the least of my brethren, you do to me." It makes Israel very uncomfortable to know we still feel the same way today.

Palestinian Christians interviewed in the piece pointed out that their suffering is the suffering of every Palestinian. Settlements, checkpoints, and racist policies strike Palestinian Christians in precisely the same manner as they do every their Muslim brethren. Every Palestinian Christian family has the same stories of imprisonment, arrest, and loss. Every Palestinian Christian feels the same devastation when he sees a new settlement raised on his olive groves. Every Palestinian Christian experiences the same revulsion when Israeli cookbooks contain recipes for stuffed grape leaves, baklava, and hummus. Every Palestinian Christian bears the same humiliation when he tries to move freely in his own land. If I thought being Christian would get me through a checkpoint any quicker, I'd wear the biggest cross I could find. I'm going to sing Christmas carols next time I arrive in Tel Aviv. I don't think if it will help, but I'm willing to try anything at this point.

In modern Palestinian history, Palestinian Christians have been at the forefront of our struggle. Edward Said, our foremost voice for over 30 years until his death in 2003, was a Christian. The Palestinian National Conservatory of Music is named after him. Azmi Bishara, a Palestinian Christian citizen of Israel, was a member of the Israeli Knesset until 2007 when he resigned amid accusations that he was aiding and abetting Hizbollah. The Israeli government passed a special law stripping him of his pension. He now lives in exile. The mayor of Ramallah, Palestine's de facto capital and center of political activity, is a Palestinian Christian woman, Janet Mikhail. Hanan Ashrawi, another Palestinian Christian woman, has been a leading activist and politician in Palestine for her whole life, standing at times in opposition to the Palestinian Authority and Yasser Arafat. She still lives and works tirelessly in Palestine. Alex Odeh was a Palestinian Christian who spoke out for Palestinians right here in America. In 1985, he was killed in California by a bomb planted by members of the Jewish Defense League. His killers were identified by the FBI and now live freely in Israel. On the day of his murder, he was scheduled to speak at a synagogue.

And, of course, there's that one Palestinian Christian who started it all. Like us, he walked the streets of Nazareth, Bethlehem, and Jerusalem, in constant persecution. He said it 2000 years ago, and we say it again today: Beware of our Truth.

64 years and we're still here

It's May 15 again, and we are still here. We haven't gone anywhere. Though, if you've been watching the news lately, you might think we no longer exist. We are nowhere to be found on the airwaves of CNN these days. It's not like we haven't been doing anything. Hundreds of Palestinian prisoners have been participating in a hunger strike for almost three months in protest of horrendous conditions and administrative detention in Israeli jails. So just in case you were wondering... We're still here.

We Palestinians are persistent. We tell our story to whoever will listen. In fact, we'll even tell it when no one wants to listen. You can't meet a Palestinian without hearing those magic words in the first few minutes: "In 1948..." We always let you know... We're still here.

Palestinians live in every corner of the world. And wherever we live, we do well. We succeed. See, we've been robbed of our homeland, dignity, and history. So we make up for it by being smarter than everyone else. We go to school and get professional degrees, even if we only plan on becoming a comedian. We don't just work in the gas station, we own it. We don't just work in the hospital, we run it. We don't just teach at the university, we manage the department. And we don't just tell jokes, we try to make you think a little bit too. What I'm trying to say is... We're still here.

To Israelis, we are a recurring nightmare, a constant reminder of the price of their "independence." They know we're present, but they don't like to talk about it. They don't even like to call us Palestinians. They'd rather call us "Arabs"... as in, they'd rather we lived in any other Arab country. In 1948, over 700,000 of us were displaced, including my one-month old father. Those 700,000 are now over 4.6 million. My dad had 4 children, and most Palestinians think that's a small family! Do the math... We're still here.

In Israel, hundreds of thousands of Palestinians are classified as "present absentees." I know, it sounds weird, like "deafening silence," "invisible ink," or "Israeli justice." Sometimes, they even call us "internally displaced." That's who we

74

are... Presently absent internally displaced victims of Israeli justice. But however you look at it... We're still here.

Hummus, falafel, baba ghanouj, and stuffed grape leaves are all staples of Israeli cuisine. Israelis might not like us, but they love our food. I can't blame them. I remember I used to bring my white friends over to my house for dinner when I was a kid. They couldn't get enough of my mom's cooking. Well, Palestine let some white people come over, and they loved her cooking too. I let my white friends sleep over every now and then, but they eventually went home. No such luck in Palestine. In any case, every time one of Palestine's white friends enjoys a falafel sandwich, filled with Palestinian lettuce, Palestinian pickles, and that tasty Palestinian tahini sauce, he can't help but to remember one thing... We're still here.

Hitting the Palestinian punching bag again

August 2, 2012

Look, as a Palestinian, I'm used to hearing racist and inhumane phrases thrown my way. Benjamin Netanyahu labels us a "demographic threat." Yitzhak Rabin told Israeli soldiers to "break the bones" of Palestinians protesting during the first Intifada. And famously, Golda Meir once even told the world, "There is no such thing as a Palestinian people... It's not as if we came and threw them out... They didn't exist."

In the past few years, this trend has made its way firmly into American politics. Of course, we've had to constantly deal with American politicians speaking of Israeli and American "shared values" and Israel's special status as the Middle East's "lone democracy." Back when Barack Obama was running for president in 2008, he was accused of having a "Palestinian friend." Obama grudgingly confirmed the fact, but urged reporters to not make him a victim of "guilt by association."

I started to think that we Palestinians were somehow scary. I was worried we would end up in haunted houses right next to the ghosts and zombies. Wait, forget I said that. I don't want to give anyone any ideas!

In this 2012 presidential race, we are at the forefront again. Last December, Newt Gingrich called us "invented." I didn't know exactly how to take that one.

At that time, Newt was pleasing his financier, Jewish-American casino magnate Sheldon Adelson, who had donated millions to his fledgling campaign. Well, now Newt is gone (kinda), and Mitt Romney is taking his turn to cozy up to Adelson, in hopes of padding his own campaign coffers.

A few days ago, with Adelson in the audience at a $50,000-a-plate breakfast in Jerusalem, Romney hit all the talking points, bashing Iran and speaking of an "undivided Jerusalem." But like many candidates vying for the backing of Israel's supporters, he didn't stop there. He went on to say the large discrepancy between GDPs in Israel and the territories managed by the Palestinian Authority was due to cultural differences and the "hand of providence." I don't want to put

76

words in Romney's idiotic mouth, but it sounds like he was saying Palestinians are bad businessman (because they're Palestinian) and that God is on Israel's side.

I don't know whose side God is on (if he's taking sides at all), but I can say with some authority that Palestinians are pretty gifted at business. Aside from building many successful ventures in the West Bank, despite a strangling Israeli occupation that stifles growth and creates a complete dependence on Israeli goods, Palestinians are pretty good when it comes to business dealings of all kinds. I've seen my dad buy a car, and I'm pretty sure the salesman called his mom for comfort after the deal was done.

Romney went on to defend his remarks, saying that the main cultural feature that allows an economy to prosper is freedom. He's probably right about that. And undoubtedly, there's little to no freedom in the West Bank and Gaza. I wonder if he knows why that is so. It's almost as if he doesn't watch the news or read any books. We already had one oblivious and illiterate president. We don't need another one.

Romney, in a recently published editorial defending his remarks, noted that America had a successful economy because Americans are not "limited by circumstance of birth nor directed by the supposedly informed hand of government." Well, we Palestinians (in both Israel and the occupied territories) are limited by the circumstances of our birth. But it's not our fault. And we are directed by the supposedly informed hand of government. But it's not our own government. And that's not our fault either.

Mr. Romney, you're right. Freedom is the key. You are free to unequivocally support Israel. You are free to say you would move the US embassy to Jerusalem. You're free to applaud Israel's "democracy." You're even free to sell yourself to the highest bidder.

But you're not allowed to be dumb.

When will Palestinians become human?

August 29, 2012

We Palestinians have been struggling for a long time. I am not speaking of the struggle to be recognized as an independent state, or the struggle to be recognized in the United Nations, or even the struggle to be recognized in international courts. I am speaking, rather, of the struggle to be recognized as human beings.

I am a comedian, and I travel to Israel and Palestine often to perform, visit, and conduct workshops. I have, to this point, done all of my work for Palestinian audiences and participants. My first job is to be funny. But I also hope to show that Palestinians can laugh just like everyone else, especially at ourselves. If I do my job well, maybe I can show that we can be funny too.

The legal decision handed down yesterday in Israel, absolving the government of any and all responsibility in the 2003 death of American Rachel Corrie in Gaza, confirmed something to the world that we Palestinians are already acutely aware of: We, and those who dare to stand with us, are simply not recognized as human beings.

In the past few weeks, this phenomenon has become all too clear in Israel. On August 16, a group of teenagers beat a Palestinian boy to near death in a Jerusalem city square. One of those arrested for that crime publicly declared his astonishment for being held accountable for beating an Arab. On that same day, a taxi carrying a family of Palestinians was firebombed near Hebron in the southern West Bank. Six Palestinians were injured in that attack.

Rachel Corrie was killed while she was decrying the demolition of homes in the Gaza Strip. She was engaging in something that we Americans have been politically and socially bred to have pride in: non-violent protest. She stood in front of a bulldozer, only to have the driver run her over, viewing her life as no more worthy than the owners of the house he was destroying.

It is no small thing to say that the state of Israel views Palestinians as subhuman. I do not say it lightly. I have traveled to Israel many times, encountering the various checkpoints, border crossings, and security personnel. I am always shocked by how Palestinians deal with this everyday. Sadly, however, I am never shocked by the subhuman manner in which Israel treats them.

The Qalandia checkpoint from Ramallah to Jerusalem is ornamented with cages and steel revolving door contraptions. Palestinians are let through at the whim of the Israeli soldiers manning the stations. The checkpoint itself is filthy and unsanitary. Similarly, Arab towns inside Israel are many times dilapidated, almost completely neglected by the Israeli government, while Jewish towns are generously funded and kept up, resembling upscale American suburbs. Studies have shown that the Israeli government spends three times more on schools populated by Jewish students than it does on schools populated by Arab students.

Prime Minister Benjamin Netanyahu once referred to the Palestinian citizens of Israel as a "demographic threat." That remark is, of course, utterly racist. But one has to wonder how someone like Mr. Netanyahu, who graduated from both high school and college in America, could refer to a group of people that existed in that land for centuries before the establishment of Israel as a "demographic threat." The answer is simple: Palestinians are simply not human.

Newt Gingrich has called us "invented," Barack Obama was attacked in 2008 for having a "Palestinian friend," Ehud Barak referred to us as "crocodiles," and former Prime Minister Menachem Begin, who famously made peace with Egypt, said that Palestinians were "beasts." Why would we expect Israel to hold anyone responsible for killing a young woman foolish enough to try to protect the rights of these creatures?

Bibi entertains us at the UN

September 29, 2012

This week, Benjamin Netanyahu delivered a speech in front of the General Assembly of the United Nations. As a Palestinian, I tuned in. It's my duty. Plus, I say the guy's name at least 3-4 times a day (I won't tell you how or why), so the least I could do was to listen to his speech.

He started innocently enough, referring to how Israel is the ancestral homeland of the Jewish people, as well as their deep history and acumen. No problem. He called Jerusalem Israel's "eternal capital." Whatever. He said the Jewish people will "never be uprooted again." Fine. "We restored our independence," he said. Well, Israel wanting to "restore" its independence from 3000 years ago is kind of like me saying I'd like to "restore" my girlfriend from college. It might sound nice, but she married someone else.

But I always knew that Benjamin Netanyahu was a proud Israeli who used history to make political points. So there was nothing surprising here.

Then Bibi began to describe the current war between the "modern and the medieval." He told us that modernity "seeks a bright future in which the rights of all are protected," while medievalism seeks to "suppress knowledge" and "glorify death." He spoke of Israeli inventions and praised Israeli innovation. I will note, as my dad constantly reminded me, that the medieval Islamic world did invent algebra, chemistry, universities, chess, shampoo, surgery, numbers, and coffee. Yes, Starbucks is entirely our fault. Oh, and we invented flying carpets, so take that!

Of course, according to him, the war between modernity and medievalism is most "stark" in the Middle East, and Israel is, of course, on the side of modernity. Translation: Jews, good... Arabs, Muslims, bad.

I always knew Bibi didn't like Arabs and Muslims. It's actually a job requirement for any Israeli prime minister. So there was nothing shocking here.

Netanyahu then delved into the Palestinian-Israeli peace process. In order to solve the conflict, he told us all parties should avoid "libelous speeches" and "unilateral declarations." But he has repeatedly called us a "demographic threat."

80

That's pretty defamatory, mister. Israel "unilaterally" pulled out of Gaza and blockaded it. It "unilaterally" built more settlements and "unilaterally" united Jerusalem. It even "unilaterally" declared hummus the Israeli national snack! I don't remember any negotiations about that.

He also said, "We have to sit together, negotiate together, and reach a mutual compromise, in which a demilitarized Palestinian state recognizes the one and only Jewish State." It kind of sounds like he's already decided the outcome of the "mutual compromise." And why did he say it's the "one and only" Jewish state? Is anyone else making a claim?

But I always knew Bibi held monumental double standards when it came to Palestinians and Israelis. So none of that stuff startled me.

But he couldn't stop talking about those backward Muslims. He told us that "the medieval forces of radical Islam" want to "end the modern world," namely Israel, Europe, and America. Perhaps he doesn't know that those Arabs and Muslims hold a party whenever they get a visa to the United States. And if they get a green card, they set off fireworks. Maybe he thinks they're just having one last big strategy session before they set sail, getting one final lesson on explosives.

He compared radical Islam to the Nazis. Now that's just unfair. Muslims don't have any kind of universal hand gestures, unless you count that circular hand motion they make when they're fighting about who should go through the door first.

Then he started talking about nuclear weapons and Iran. "To understand what the world would be like with a nuclear-armed Iran, just imagine the world with a nuclear-armed Al-Qaeda." Really? Al-Qaeda? We're supposed to believe the group that conducts military exercises on a playground could build a nuclear weapon? They can't even run a good boot camp.

And let's be real. Al-Qaeda is not doing that well. Every week CNN tells me, "Today, a military strike killed al-Qaeda's number two man." There's really no job security in that organization.

He spoke of how close Iran is to making a nuclear bomb, and how the world must act now to stop them. Then he claimed to know how close Iran is to achieving its goal of world destruction.

Then Bibi said, "I brought a diagram." Now this was different. Israelis are not known for diagrams. They usually hate maps and annoying things like borders. This was totally new for me. I started to get interested.

Now I always thought Netanyahu was a little imbalanced, but I didn't think he was completely insane until he held up a Road Runner-like drawing of a circle with a squiggly black line coming out of it and said, "This is a bomb, this is a fuse." But I have to call Bibi out on this lie as well. I'm an Arab, and I can tell you with some authority, that is not what a bomb looks like.

Of course, Bibi actually knows exactly what a bomb looks like. And he knows what a nuclear bomb looks like too. It is estimated that Israel could have up to 400 nuclear bombs in its arsenal. But the "only democracy in the Middle East" has a policy of "opacity" when it comes to its nuclear program. In other words, no one gets to know anything about Israel's nuclear program, but everyone has to know everything about Iran's.

Israel has refused to sign the Nuclear Non-Proliferation Treaty. And in case anyone was wondering, every state in the "modern" world has signed it. In fact, almost every "medieval" Islamic nation has signed it too.

I have an important piece of paper I'd like to show the prime minster of Israel. And there's something I need to tell him about it:

This is a treaty. This is where you sign it.

Israel, stop stealing our stuff!

October 13, 2012

The life of a Palestinian can be pretty depressing. We have to deal with dispossession and the refugee life. Then there's all the racism. And don't forget the media misrepresentation, military occupation, checkpoints, and seizure of resources. Being Palestinian is relentless. There are no breaks. Just when it looks like everything's OK, someone calls us "invented," or "barbaric," or "resentful," or "hateful." Those of us in Palestine have to deal with daily humiliation. Those of us everywhere else have to deal with daily explaining. "Have you heard of Theodore Herzl? Or the Balfour Declaration? Resolution 194? OK, sit down, I'm gonna make coffee."

But the worst part of being Palestinian, by far, is watching Israelis steal our stuff. I don't mean stealing our land, demolishing homes, and building settlements. Yeah, all of that is bad. But I'm talking about the theft of our stuff... our scenery, our architecture, and our history. Nothing makes me angrier than seeing an Israeli tanning on a Tel Aviv beach, smoking a hookah. And don't forget about the theft of our recipes. I don't even want to tell you how many Jewish girls I've had to dump over hummus. Being Palestinian means having to watch Israelis constantly pretend they are us.

If you don't believe that Israelis are trying to be like us, just go back and watch Benjamin Netanyahu's speech at the UN a couple weeks ago. He was rambling, spouting conspiracy theories, promoting his own cultural superiority, and talking as if he was brilliant and everyone else was dumb. Need I say more?

I've always said that we Palestinians are contagious. I've never wanted to find a cure until now.

Last week, I was watching one of my favorite shows, "Homeland." For those who might not watch it, the show is about America's war against terrorism. Specifically, it focuses on the CIA's attempts to kill or capture the head of some crazy Islamic terrorist organization called "Al-Qaeda." At first, I was offended, but then I discovered that the show's main plotline also features a white American terrorist, so that made me feel a lot better. But then I found out he converted to Islam. Dammit!

83

Anyway, last week's episode featured an assassination attempt on Abu Nazir, the fictional Al-Qaeda leader in "Homeland." The CIA had tracked him to Beirut, and was geared to take him out. Abu Nazir survived because the white terrorist guy in the show, who is also a congressman, tipped him off. Yes, the show has a lot of twists and turns. The scenery was great and looked strikingly authentic. Afterwards, I thought, "Wow, I wonder how an American program about assassinating an Arab got permission to film in Beirut."

Well, my question was immediately answered. After the show concluded, Showtime aired a short "behind the scenes" segment about the attempted assassination. I quickly learned that the dramatic scene was not filmed in Beirut. Instead, it was filmed right down the road in Haifa, in Israel. The director explained how Haifa was the perfect stand-in for Beirut because of its "textures" and "Arabic face."

I'm sure the producers of American-made "Homeland" had no problem getting permission from the Israeli Culture Ministry's film commission to film there. $5 billion a year should get us Americans certain privileges. I mean, I don't get any privileges when I go there, but whatever.

I can just imagine the conversation between the director of "Homeland" and the head of Israel's film commission:

Director: Hi, we're looking for a place with an Arab feel where we almost kill an Islamic terrorist.
Israel: Almost kill? We'd be happy to give you lessons.
Director: No, it's fake... we're shooting a TV show, and we need a place that looks like Beirut.
Israel: Well, you know we are a western democracy with western culture and ideals, right?
Director: Yeah, of course.
Israel: Then why are you calling us?
Director: Well, I just thought...
Israel: Ha ha, just kidding, you need an Arab-looking city, right?
Director: Yeah.
Israel: No problem, we have lots of those... I'll send you a list.

Hey Bill O'Reilly, where are the moderate Jews?

October 26, 2012

Where is Bill O'Reilly when you need him?

This week, Israeli newspaper Haaretz published a survey that contained some shocking findings. According to journalist Gideon Levy, who penned the article for Haaretz, "The survey indicates that a third to half of Jewish Israelis want to live in a state that practices formal, open discrimination against its Arab citizens. An even larger majority wants to live in an apartheid state if Israel annexes the territories."

Bill, are you listening? You're famous for speaking of a "Muslim dilemma." You and many other commentators have pleaded for reasonable, moderate Muslims to make their voices heard in the face of Islamic extremism and movements that devalue the lives and status of non-Muslims.

Moderate, peace-loving Muslims have populated your show and many others, usually bombarded by your insistence that they denounce extremism. And you are convincing. Arab and Muslim groups always send out condemning press releases distancing themselves whenever an extremist group or individual does something crazy.

Well, now we have a nation, one that claims to speak for the entire Jewish people, that has unmasked its beliefs in a pretty extreme fashion.

Israeli study: 59% of Israeli Jews favor preference for Jews over Arabs in admission to government jobs.

Bill, where are the moderate Jewish voices?

Israeli study: 49% of Israeli Jews want the state to treat Jewish citizens better than Arab ones.

Bill, aren't you outraged?

Israeli study: 42% of Israeli Jews don't want to live in the same building as Arabs.

Well, this is ridiculous, right? I know the smell of garlic from the kitchen can be overwhelming, but on the bright side, you'll get invited to dinner at least 3 times a week.

Israeli study: 42% of Israeli Jews don't want their kids in the same classroom as Arabs.

Bill, we Americans outlawed segregation in schools a long time ago. Remember? These backwards Israelis are revolting. Now, Israel already funds Jewish schools three times more than it funds Arab schools. But that's ok. We invented algebra and chemistry, so we can do without education.

Israeli study: 74% of Israeli Jews favor separate roads for Jews and Arabs in the West Bank.

OK, I have driven alongside Arabs in the Middle East, and I would rather skydive without a parachute. So I totally understand this one.

Israeli study: 33% of Israeli Jews would support a law banning Israeli Arab citizens from voting.

Bill, this one even makes the KKK jealous.

Mr. O'Reilly, shouldn't reasonable, moderate Jews speak up?! Bring me on the show. Let's talk about it!

No Jewish-American group, to my knowledge, has made any public statement about this troubling study. When Muslim and Arab American groups fail to denounce extremist views and acts, we are labeled as "complicit." Bill, it's safe to assume that American Jews concur with these racist views prevalent in Israeli society, right? If not, where are the moderate voices?

Of course, the sad irony is that American Jews, who have honorably been at the forefront civil rights struggles here, are usually all too silent when it comes to Israel.

To a Palestinian, the results of this survey are not too surprising. As Arab Knesset member Jamal Zahalka noted, "We're talking about racism, pure and simple. The Israeli regime isn't a carbon copy of South Africa's apartheid, but it is certainly from the same family." We have long lived in a world where we know the Israeli state is built upon the notion that Jews are simply better than Arabs. In that world, Jews are human beings worthy of rights and Arabs are not. Separate roads, separate schools, and institutionalized racism are not memories of an ugly past. They are realities of a hideous present.

Mr. O'Reilly, you once asserted, "For every Muslim in the world who wants democracy and human rights, there's one who doesn't." That would be a scary ratio. But there are no studies to prove those statistics. Who would have ever thought that you could have said the exact same thing about Israelis and been exactly right?

Explaining being Palestinian

How do I explain who we are?

We wake up every morning with a hole in our heart, for a homeland dispossessed, a history stolen, and a future trampled. We live knowing that something is missing, and fearing that it will never return.

I'm going to try to explain it you. I hope you understand.

We turn on the news just to see what they're saying about us. We are never happy about it. Our friends might yell at the TV while watching the NFL. We yell while watching CNN.

It's hard to explain, and even harder to understand.

When we have some time to ourselves, our grandmother's stories ring in our ears. We try to imagine them in happier times, living in Yafa, Haifa, and Jerusalem, meticulously tending to their houses, rolling grape leaves, and readying a pot of coffee. But we cannot help then seeing them driven from those same homes that had been in their families for generations, becoming hopeless refugees in lands where they did not belong. We cannot help seeing them going from working as teachers to working as maids, from living in comfort to living in poverty, from sounding proud to sounding broken. And we cannot help but to imagine some other family, seizing that beautiful home, with its small garden, herbal scents, and vibrant colors, all while the pot of coffee was still warm.

I'm trying to explain it. But it's difficult.

We have to listen to the American president say that Israel has every right to defend herself, noting, "There's no country on Earth that would tolerate missiles raining down on its citizens from outside its borders." Outside its borders? The 1.7 million people of Gaza live completely at the mercy of Israel's blockade. Aid groups cannot access the population. In fact, Israel determines what humanitarian aid can and cannot enter. That's like President Obama hiring the KKK to run the Secret Service. If someone doesn't believe that you should even exist, he probably shouldn't decide whether or not you get food, water, and medicine.

President Obama of course knows the truth, making his servitude to Israel that much more disgusting. I don't know how to explain how that feels.

88

We watch Israelis call themselves victims and us the aggressors. We live in an alternate world defined by double standards, illusions and simple ridiculousness, where our struggle against occupation and land confiscation is terrorism, where Israeli architecture is defined by arched windows and intricate colorful tiles, and where falafel, grape leaves, and hummus are staples of Israeli cuisine.

I'm trying to explain it, but am I getting the point across?

When we meet fellow Palestinians for the first time, we get excited. We exchange information and stories about our hometowns, our family names, and our journeys. We talk about all the different places we have lived, and the one place where we wish we could have. We share rage, sorrow, and despair. And even though it's hard to explain, we can't wait to see each other again.

We see reports of our devastated, impoverished brethren being bombarded by a modern, superior military. We watch in horror as young and old alike die for simply being present. We see Israeli politicians hold demonstrations chanting "There are no innocents in Gaza!"

I don't know if I can explain how it feels to know that the person holding the gun to your head sees you as a worthless animal.

I don't know if I can explain how it feels to see Israel drop a bomb and massacre an entire family, all while saying it was targeting a terrorist that no one in the neighborhood has ever heard of... or that any one of us would have traded places with the four children who were there.

This is who we are. I've tried to explain it. It might sound tragic, but don't feel bad for us. We have a connection to each other you might not ever understand. We smile and laugh more than you might think. And somehow, we still fall asleep with a heart full of warmth, justice, and hope.

When we wake up, that hole in our heart is back again. But just like you, we live another day.

Israel, what would you do without us?

Seriously, what would Israel do without us?

Israelis are struggling with their identity, with their future. Mainly they're asking themselves a core question: What are we finally going to do with all these Palestinians?

Israel is holding elections on Tuesday, and the debate seems to be between those on the right and those on the far right. In other words, the decision is between maintaining the status quo (the occupation of the West Bank and the blockade of Gaza) and fully settling and incorporating the West Bank. Of course, these questions wouldn't exist if we just weren't around.

If it weren't for us, I don't know what they would talk about.

The debates in Israel are lively. Now, they don't directly talk about it, but everything centers on us Palestinians. We make Israeli life exciting. So to my Israeli friends, I say: You're welcome!

If it weren't for us, CNN wouldn't care much about Israel. A country full of one kind of people not causing any uproar in the UN wouldn't be that stimulating. If Israel had actually been founded on a vacant land, the New York Times would never write about it. But because of us, you get headlines every day. You're welcome.

If it weren't for us, there would no Israeli lobby, wielding unmatched power and influence on Capitol Hill. Your impact here is impressive. You can actually cause US senators to consider rejecting a decorated Vietnam Veteran's appointment to head the Defense Department. That kind of sway can only come about because we are part of the conversation. You're welcome.

If it weren't for us, you definitely wouldn't be getting $5 billion a year from American taxpayers. You might get something, but not $5 billion. You might have to fund your own army, your own cities, and your own political campaigns. You know they don't give you that money because of that "shared value" nonsense, right? It's because you've been able to convince them, quite successfully, that we (and anyone who looks

90

like us) want to wipe you off of the face of the earth. We're the reason you're able to get that big check. So, you're welcome.

If it weren't for us, Iran would never say anything about you. You wouldn't be able to go the UN, hold up signs of a cartoonish bomb, educating diplomats what a fuse looks like. It's because of us you were able to conduct that seminar. I know you won't thank us, but you're welcome anyway.

And it would be unjust for me not to mention our contributions to your cuisine. Every Israeli cookbook I read (yes, I pick them up whenever I get a chance) contains recipes for falafel, hummus, and stuffed grape leaves. We brought garlic into your lives. It does a number on your breath, but you have to admit, the food is damn good. You don't even have to thank me for this one. Everyone loves our food. You're welcome.

If it weren't for us, people might notice that you were rallying against the presence of black people in your country. And that kind of stuff does not go over well here in America. Trust me. We're having an inauguration, and our president sort of looks like those people you're demonstrating against. We actually have a federal holiday for a black guy. But you can turn all the attention to us whenever you need to. We should get a big thank you for this one. You are welcome.

If it weren't for us, what would you do? What would you talk about? You might have to learn to live without conflict. I've been watching you for a long time. And from what I've seen, I'm not sure you can do that.

Lucky for you, we're not going anywhere, and we're pretty loud, so you should be fine for some time to come. From my people to yours, you're welcome.

And just so you know, I'm open to a "thank you" every now and then. If you feel the urge to send a card, please do. You can reach me in Nazareth, Haifa, Jaffa, Ramallah, or Bethlehem. I also have an address in Gaza, but the mail doesn't always get there safely. But if it's easier for you, you can just send it to my mailbox in Jerusalem. I check that one the most.

91

Bill Maher, welcome to the club!

February 19, 2013

On Friday night, live on national TV, Bill Maher said:

Based on every statement I've heard from every Republican in the last two years, the Israelis are controlling our government.

I thought for a second that I was in a dream. See, when we Arabs hear something like that said openly on American TV, we literally jump out of our seats.

Based on every statement I've heard from every Republican in the last two years, the Israelis are controlling our government.

We start looking around for the hidden cameras.

Based on every statement I've heard from every Republican in the last two years, the Israelis are controlling our government.

We call our parents, our siblings, and our friends. We send mass texts, we tweet... we even start Facebook groups.

Based on every statement I've heard from every Republican in the last two years, the Israelis are controlling our government.

I actually went out to my front porch and started singing:

The hills are alive with the sound of music!

Unfortunately, it's definitely true that not too many Arab-Americans saw you on Friday night on HBO. We don't pay for anything more than basic cable TV unless it's Al-Jazeera. But the quote and its accompanying video quickly made it around our circles. And we welcome you with open arms.

Now, of course you were responding to one of your panelists, right-wing blogger Jamie Weinstein, who brought up a Chuck Hagel speech where the former senator said that Israel

92

was controlling some branches of our government. And so you said what you said.

And you're right, in that it seems that Israel and its American lobby group, AIPAC, do control the Republican Party when it comes to Middle East politics. The whole right-wing platform on the Middle East is basically a carbon copy of what Benjamin Netanyahu says every day. This includes a passionate fixation with Iran, supporting increased settlement construction in the West Bank and East Jerusalem, and a basic rejection of the Palestinians and their rights to liberty and self-determination. It also includes Republican politicians uttering nonsensical things about us Palestinians, saying that we are hateful, resentful, devoid of culture, and "invented."

And, of course, it means continuing the unrestricted backing and funding of the Israeli military occupation of the West Bank and the blockade of the Gaza Strip.

Yes, I said "occupation." I bring that up because, as you might remember, I was once a guest on your former program, "Politically Incorrect." In fact, I was twice a guest. Actually, I was going to be on a third time, but then you got kicked off the air for some post-9/11 comments, ruining my dream of becoming a talking head.

When I visited you in December 2001 and April 2002, we talked about the Palestinian-Israeli conflict. And I must say, at that time, you didn't sound too different from the right-wing Republicans who unconditionally and blindly support Israel today.

Back then, you hated the word "occupation." Every time I would use it, you would say there was no such thing. You repudiated references to an "occupation" by the United Nations and other international legal bodies. When you said "the occupied land," you actually used air quotes.

You insisted that Israel was just a lonely little democracy, surrounded by a sea of Arab neighbors that were waiting for the right moment to annihilate it.

You claimed that it was solely the Arabs who rejected the UN partition plan in 1947. I said that most probably both the Arabs and the Israelis disliked it, especially based on a new brand of Israeli academics calling themselves the "New Historians." I said they existed. You said that was "so not true."

You maintained that the Palestinian refugees should just be absorbed into neighboring Arab lands. You said that Israel could not allow the right of return because it would harm the Jewish character of the state.

93

You said that 1967 was the year that the Arabs attacked Israel (so not true).

You said that the media is not biased toward Israel. "I think the media is biased toward the Palestinians," you pronounced.

You basically towed the right-wing Israeli, GOP line regarding Israel, complete with all the Netanyahu-approved talking points.

But that was a long time ago, and I have been watching you since. You have mellowed. You have started to exit the alternate universe inhabited by Israel and its supporters and enter the reality lived by us Palestinians. I'd love to come back and talk about it.

When I was on your show, I was wearing glasses, and I had a full head of hair. I don't wear glasses anymore. I don't wear hair anymore either.

I guess time can change everything.

I can't escape being Palestinian!

March 4, 2013

Being a Palestinian is relentless. It's action-packed, hectic, and lively. It's frantic, frenzied, and chaotic. It's frenetic, feverish, and downright wild. Those are all the appropriate words I could find in the thesaurus on Microsoft Word.

But don't worry, I'm used to it.

The past couple weeks have been especially eventful. It started with the excitement we all felt knowing that a Palestinian-made film was nominated for an Oscar. "5 Broken Cameras" is about how the Palestinian residents of Bil'in mounted a non-violent campaign against the Israeli separation wall cutting through their village, threatening their land ownership rights and livelihoods. It follows director Emad Burnat, a self-taught cameraman, as he documents his village's resistance efforts through the lenses of five different cameras, each of which gets destroyed sometime along the way.

A Palestinian nominated for an Oscar? Cool. Maybe this would be a good week. Emad Burnat would come to America and represent our struggle, tell the world that we Palestinians love peace just as much as anyone, and let everyone know that we have the right to demand our rights, that we are human beings. He would come to America and do all those things. If he could get in, that is. Upon Emad's arrival to Los Angeles International Airport, US immigration agents detained him (remember, he's an Oscar nominee). It's not going to be a good week. No other foreign Oscar nominees were detained, just the Palestinian. I'm not saying Emad got profiled, but... Ok, I'm saying he got profiled.

Of course, now I had to watch the Oscars. I didn't really plan to watch the show, but I got together with some old Palestinian friends and sat through a couple hours of awards about editing and visual effects. Finally it was time for "Best Documentary." I don't know why I held out hope. We Palestinians didn't win. We were robbed... again.

I needed to escape my Palestinian-ness for a while. There would be no better time than my flight to Houston for a show. When the crew asked us to turn off our phones, I quickly finished my game of solitaire and grabbed a copy of the United

95

Airlines magazine, "Hemispheres." My escape would be short-lived. Inside, I read the following cover headline:

MEET THE ROWDY REVOLUTIONARY CHEFS WHO ARE SHAKING UP ISRAELI CUISINE

Oh, Jesus. I didn't want to read the article, but I was Palestinian-ly required to do so. The first line didn't help to relieve my tension:

Settled by Jews from places as diverse as Eastern Europe, North Africa, and the Middle East, Israel is a nation of immigrants.

C'mon. Did this really have to happen to me? I was relaxed, my seatbelt was fastened, and I was following instructions. I'm a good person. I was ready to start a fun weekend. "A nation of immigrants"? I tend to think of immigrants as people who swim across a river or jump over a fence. I don't tend to think of them as people with tanks and helicopters building concrete walls through other people's villages.

The next line of the article helped a little bit:

Yet for all the country's international flavor, what's long been characteristic Israeli food – hummus, falafel, mixed grilled meats, fresh chopped salads – is in fact cuisine borrowed from local Levantines.

"Borrowed" is a nice way of putting it, but I'll take it. That admission only took 64 years, 9 months, and 27 days... but who's counting?

Then just yesterday I woke up to find out that an Israeli bus company has decided to run "Palestinian-only" lines. Afikim is an Israeli bus company, contracted by the Israeli government to operate bus service from the West Bank into Israel. It mostly serves settlers, but it also serves some of the 29,000 Palestinian residents of the West Bank who hold permits to work inside Israel. The separate bus line was created after Israeli settlers residing inside the West Bank complained that they didn't feel "safe" with Palestinian riders alongside them. Legalized segregation was done away with in America almost 60 years ago. Israel is going retro. She's bringing it back!

Now, we should be clear that this is not about security, just like it wasn't about security in Alabama in 1955. How do I know it's not about security? During the month of Ramadan in 2012, 1.2 million Palestinians from the West Bank entered

96

Israel. They shopped, dined, and partied. They gave a noticeable bump to the Israeli economy. They flooded Israel's beaches. Yeah, they swam fully clothed, but it was Ramadan after all. 1.2 million of them. And guess what? No attacks. Zero. The bus segregation is about something, but it's definitely not about security.

I wish this bus thing never occurred, but don't worry, this kind of stuff happens to me all the time.

I thought all the madness was over until this morning. I looked through my Facebook feed and found this:

Palestinian waiter assaulted by Israelis in Tel Aviv

Damn. Can't I get one day of peace? This time a Palestinian waiter was just doing his job when a group of Jewish customers started complaining. They then called him a "smelly Arab" and started hitting him and throwing tables and chairs at him. No one intervened, and police refused to file charges against the assailants, even though the incident was caught on surveillance video.

I don't know if this Palestinian lives in the West Bank. But if he does, at least he'll be safe on his bus ride home.

Barack, a few travel tips

March 13, 2013

Mr. President, I hear you are traveling to Israel next week. As a concerned patriotic American citizen of Palestinian descent, I have some pointers for you.

Now, I assume you'll be flying into Tel Aviv. Usually, when non-Jews arrive there, especially if they are a little darker-skinned, they are asked to wait in a... let's call it a "VIP Room." Incidentally, the room is quite nice. There's a water cooler, comfortable chairs, and a soda machine. It's probably the only place in the world where you can be racially profiled and get an ice-cold Coca-Cola all at once.

To avoid the room, I would mention that you are the President of the United States. It might help.

You may get strip-searched. Saying you are an American doesn't help much here. I've tried. I even sang the national anthem the last time an Israeli soldier was looking down my pants. I said, "Oh say can you see." He said, "Not much."

To escape this embarrassment, I would mention that you are the President of the United States. It might help.

In case they don't already know, you might want to kind of veil from Israeli security the fact that you are half-Muslim. As a fellow half-Muslim, I can tell you they don't really care about the percentage. Any bit of Muslim freaks them out. And I'm not sure if you heard, but the fans of one of Israel's soccer teams, Beitar Jerusalem, actually protested when the club signed two Muslim players. When one of them scored in a game last week, hundreds of fans actually walked out of the stadium. One of the fans later stated about the Muslim players, "It's not racism. They just shouldn't be here." Hopefully, they don't know your middle name is "Hussein." Maybe they didn't watch the inauguration.

In any case, I would mention that you are the President of the United States. It might help.

This next one might be a little delicate. Maybe you didn't hear, but lately there has been a little "African problem" in Israel. Over the past several years, tens of thousands immigrants from Africa, mostly from Eritrea and Sudan, have entered the "only democracy in the Middle East." Most of them are looking for work, and some are political refugees. Israel

98

has recently rounded up many of them for deportation. Oh, and by the way, they don't call them "refugees" or "migrants," they call them "infiltrators." Israelis have held numerous demonstrations in Tel Aviv, where most of the migrants live, to demand an African exodus from Israel.

And the refugees aren't the only Africans Israel seems to have a problem with. About 150,000 Israeli Jews are of Ethiopian descent. A number of news organizations reported early this year that Israeli government doctors had been giving Ethiopian Jewish women contraceptives either against their will or without their knowledge. The Israeli government admitted the practice and decided to stop it once it was reported on. See, Mr. Obama, many rabbis in Israel have questioned the "Jewishness" of Ethiopian Jews. And if you're not Jewish in Israel, well... I'd be glad to give you the full story on that someday. So they're not too crazy about their own Ethiopian citizens, and last year, Benjamin Netanyahu warned that illegal immigrants from Africa "threaten our existence as a Jewish and democratic state." I know, "Jewish" and "democratic"? It's confusing. I'll try to explain that one to you one day too, but I can't guarantee I'll be able to. But I think one thing is clear: Israel does not seem to like Africans too much.

Now I know you're not from Eritrea, Ethiopia, or Sudan, but I probably wouldn't advertise too strongly that your dad was from Kenya. This might be really hard, given your skin tone and everything, especially if you're bringing Michelle with you.

To avoid any dangers of getting deported to Nairobi, I would just keep mentioning that you are the President of the United States. It might help.

OK, finally, when you leave, Israeli security officers are going to search your bags. And they don't do it casually with a smile like our airport security here in America. They go through your stuff like a wife looking for evidence of an affair. You might remind them that you, as the President of the United States, sign their checks.

And they're going to strip search you again. Yes, on the way out too. Strip searches in Israel are "buy one, get one free." They perform the strip search in a section of the airport aside from where the normal operations are conducted. You'll run into a few of your Palestinian-American constituents when you're there. I know it's a weird place for someone to ask to take a picture with you, but don't be alarmed, for us it's just part of visiting home.

99

You don't have to mention to us, however, that you are the President of the United States. We already know. We supported you. Twice. Maybe you can return the favor.

Mr. President, you confused me

Mr. President, I very closely followed your trip to Israel this week, and I have to say, you confused me.

You visited the Church of the Nativity in Bethlehem, the birthplace of Jesus, the most famous Palestinian of all time. The church is a United Nations World Heritage Site, listed in the UN under the "State of Palestine," a designation you loudly opposed in front of the world. It must have felt weird to see something that everyone else says exists but you say doesn't. I can relate. Every day I tell myself my belly isn't actually there.

But watching from afar, I was a little confused.

I listened carefully when you gave that monumental speech in Jerusalem. You started off talking about the strong bond between Israel and America, the perseverance of the Jewish people, and their ingenuity in building a nation. You then talked about security and the constant threat of destruction that Israel lives under. You brought up Hezbollah, Syria, and Iran, the usual suspects. You also sang to the Israeli audience:

You are not alone
I am here with you
Though we're far apart
You're always in my heart

Ok, you only said the first line, but it reminded me how much I miss Michael Jackson.

Now, you did talk to us earlier in the day in Ramallah. There you told us we shouldn't ask Israel to stop building settlements and confiscating land before we return to negotiations about where our state might be one day. So, Israel gets touchy-feely speeches and we get asked to behave.

I was a little confused.

Then you said, "Peace is necessary." And you continued:

Given the demographics west of the Jordan River, the only way for Israel to endure and thrive as a Jewish and demo-

101

cratic state is through the realization of an independent and viable Palestine.

Demographics west of the Jordan River? That means us, I think. And I think it means we are reproducing quickly. Well, without a state, we don't have much else to do. You can only demonstrate so much in one day.

This sort of sounds like the whole "demographic threat" thing Israeli politicians talk about all the time. Benjamin Netanyahu must have given Ariel Sharon a high-five when you said this. Well, not literally a high-five, because Sharon... well, whatever.

Mr. President, we Americans live in a country where our values don't allow us to use race to build the identity of our citizenry. But you said, "In Israel, we see values that we share."

Forgive me if I was a little confused.

Also, I'm not sure if you noticed, but many in the Israeli audience were Palestinians. I saw a couple of my cousins on CNN. In fact, one out of every five Israeli citizens is actually a native Palestinian and not Jewish at all. How is the whole "Jewish and democratic" thing supposed to work out for them?

Forgive me if I was a little confused.

Then you said, "Peace is just." After you stated proudly how you opposed any moves by the Palestinians to achieve state-hood in the UN, you noted:

> The Palestinian people's right to self-determination and justice must also be recognized. Put yourself in their shoes... It is not fair that a Palestinian child cannot grow up in a state of her own, and lives with the presence of a foreign army that controls the movements of her parents every single day. It is not just when settler violence against Palestinians goes unpunished. It is not right to prevent Palestinians from farming their lands; to restrict a student's ability to move around the West Bank; or to displace Palestinian families from their home. Neither occupation nor expulsion is the answer. Just as Israelis built a state in their homeland, Palestinians have a right to be a free people in their own land.

It was very nice to hear about all of our rights. But what good are rights if we have to negotiate for them? What good are they if we have to wait? Put yourself in our shoes. English is technically my second language, but I think they call them "rights" because you don't have to ask for them. They're just always there.

Again, forgive me if I was a little confused.

Then you said "peace is possible" and that "negotiations will be necessary." You noted that, "Israelis must recognize that continued settlement activity is counterproductive to the cause of peace, and that an independent Palestine must be viable– that real borders will have to be drawn." Don't worry, Mr. President. Israel is taking care of the "drawing borders" things. No negotiations necessary.

Confusing, right?

There was some reason for optimism. You reminded us that, "Four years ago, I stood in Cairo in front of an audience of young people." I remember. You spoke of freedom, democracy, and economic advancement, to rousing applause and enthusiasm. That was June 2009. In January 2011, they overthrew their whole system and moved forward in a new world. I'm glad you finally gave a big speech in Israel. We Palestinians have waited 65 years... what's another eighteen months?

Finally, before you left, you convinced Benjamin Netanyahu to apologize to his Turkish counterpart for the deaths of nine Turkish nationals at the hands of the Israeli Navy in 2010. Since you're on a roll, could I ask you to request another apology from Israel? This one would be for 450 villages, 5 million refugees, and thousands of slain children.

Sadly, you'll never do that. And that leaves me the most confused of all.

A letter to my ex-girlfriend

Have you lost your mind? Seriously, when we first met, I thought you were the one I had been waiting for my whole life. Now, I don't know what I was thinking.

I let you into my life... I shared everything I had with you. You had nothing. Everything that was mine helped you make you who you are today. Oh, how we forget so easily. You've let others come between us. I know I never had any money, but you didn't have to go shack up with the richest guy around the first chance you got.

I've tried everything, letting you have more than you could've ever hoped for. I let you into my heart. You learned my deepest secrets, and then you used them all against me. How dare you?! How could I have been so stupid?

Yes, we fought a lot. Sometimes it was my fault. Sometimes it was yours. But you go around telling everyone you're always the victim, that I was the one "terrorizing" you. What a liar! How many times have I let you humiliate me around other people? Yet I kept telling everyone we were going to work everything out. Boy, was I wrong.

I'm the only one who has made any sacrifices for this relationship. Remember when I let your cousins come over and stay in the house? They still haven't left.

I go around telling everyone I'll do whatever it takes to make you happy. You pretend like I don't even exist.

We've tried to reconcile many times. I even agreed to things I knew were bad for me, just to see if it would work out. I've never known how to say "no" to you. You've had a hold on me. But no more! I'm moving on.

From now on, I don't want anything to do with you. And by the way, I got your letter saying that you wanted me to profess my love for you in front of everyone. What nerve! When you start admitting that you did me wrong, then we'll talk about that kind of stuff.

But I'll tell you something right now. You may try to forget about us, but you won't be able to. You can keep lying to yourself and everyone else, but it will catch up to you. You can try to get me out of your heart, but it will never work. I will always be a part of you. The things you did to me and the experiences we shared won't just disappear. Life doesn't work like that. One day you'll finally realize that you're better off with me in your life.

For now, though, we have to go our separate ways. Maybe you'll grow up a little bit. Maybe we can get back together one day. If we don't end up together, I hope you at least don't put anyone else through what I had to endure. It just makes me so mad. I see you making all these mistakes, and I'm afraid you won't realize it until it's too late and you're all alone.

But you know what? If that happens, you deserve it. I begged you to just accept me for who I am. Don't try to change me. I'll always be the person you fell for: fiery, protective, passionate, and full of love. How could you have not seen it all this time? We could've had something special, if you didn't go and screw it all up.

You're so full of yourself, thinking you're so perfect, thinking you never do anything wrong. Take a look in the mirror. All of this is your fault. All you had to do was open your heart... and share a little.

I've known, for some time now, that the only future I have is with you. When will you realize it too? Stop denying it.

I let you into my life. I let you share everything I had. Before I met you, I was a virgin. I know... it's hard to believe. Well, you'll never be getting any of this Palestinian lovin' ever again. And trust me, you'll want it!

I can't believe I introduced you to my family. They told me something wasn't right, but I wouldn't listen. My mom even shared her secret family hummus recipe with you, and now you go around telling everyone it's your own... YOU B#$%H!

Go figure out your problems on your own. We'll see if you can do it without me! Don't call me. Don't text me. Don't e-mail me. I can't wait to change my Facebook relationship status. Just stay out of my life!

Screw you, Israel.
Sincerely, Palestine

105

65 years later, & we're winning

May 15, 2013

Well, it's that time of year. It's the day when we Palestinians commemorate the establishment of the state of Israel. They call it "independence," and we call it "Nakba," the Arabic word for "catastrophe."

There are still many people living today who suffered the "Nakba" of 1948, being driven from their homes, destined to become lifelong refugees. They have suffered, and they still live to tell their stories.

I even know some of these Palestinian mothers, and some of their sons never got married. Don't worry, nothing happened to their sons. They just never found the right woman. These women have suffered two Nakbas.

But as I keep thinking about the past 65 years, I have realized something very important:

We're winning!

Sure, our lives are messed up, but believe me, we're winning.

See, the Nakba was about getting rid of all the Palestinians. Now, you have to give the Israelis some credit. They tried their best, and they're still trying. But even today, 65 years later, we're more present than ever.

We're winning.

Israelis stole our food. But I'm not mad anymore. It's a compliment. I mean, you don't steal something unless it's awesome. Today, Israeli cuisine consists of hummus, falafel, and stuffed grape leaves.

We're winning.

White European Israeli Jews sit on the beaches of Haifa and Tel Aviv, taking in the Palestinian sun. They smoke hookahs. And they eat sunflower seeds and the throw the shells on the ground. They're just like us!

We're winning.

I have been to Israeli nightclubs. The DJs play techno beats infused with Arabic music. Israelis are even dancing like us. They're changing the light bulb and doing the windshield wipers!

We're winning.

I've been a guest at many Israeli checkpoints and border crossings. Sometimes, I even hang out there for many hours. When I'm there long enough to witness a shift change, I've seen how the soldiers interact with each other. They speak mostly Hebrew, but they greet each other in Arabic and use slang Arabic words. They really like "ahlan," which means "hello," "keefak," which means "how are you," and "sababa," which means "cool."

I've even heard the following conversation:

Soldier 1: Ahlan, keefak?
Soldier 2: Good.
Soldier 1: Anything exciting today?
Soldier 2: Yeah, I strip searched 35 Palestinians and turned back 5 ambulances.
Soldier 1: Sababa.

We're totally winning.

Now, Nakba day does conjure up some pain too. It makes me realize how damaged we Palestinians have become. No other people do some of the things we do.

I remember last time I was in Palestine, a friend of mine introduced me to a friend of hers. She said, "Amer, this is my friend Ahmed. He is a great man. He is the best man I have ever met in my life. He was in jail 10 years."

No one else talks like that.

Normal parents have to explain to their kids where babies come from. Palestinian parents need to explain to their kids where Israel comes from. "Well son, when America loves a group of people so much that she doesn't want them to immigrate there, they make another country."

It would be nice to compare the birth of Israel to the birth of a child, except when a baby is born, he usually doesn't punch another baby in the face as he enters the world.

On my last trip, as I was leaving Ben Gurion Airport to return to America, I got the normal treatment. I like to call it "elevated customer service." I don't get offended by all the extra profiling. It makes me feel much more significant than I actually am. And since we Palestinians are generally depressed, it actually lifts my spirits to know that at least someone thinks I'm important.

In any case, when we Palestinians leave Israel, we get a friendly strip search. It happens in a section of the airport where they have set up a bunch of dressing rooms with privacy curtains. The solider who was assigned to strip search me

107

was a very nice young man, about 22 or 23 years old. We can call him my "stripper." As we made our way over to the dressing rooms, my stripper realized that all of them were being used. I guess lots of Palestinians were leaving Israel that day. It was a good day for business.

But my stripper was clearly irritated. He just wanted to do his job and get it over with. As we waited for a room to open up, we stood against the wall. He looked over at me and muttered in frustration, "Akh, everything here is occupied."

I said, "I know how you feel."

See, Israelis are starting to feel our frustration. C'mon, how can you not think we're winning?

Israel is not doing very well. None of her neighbors like her. She can't decide if she's happy being fat or if she's happy being skinny. And she has a major case of denial, especially around this time of the year. To make things worse, in the midst of all of this, the population of Palestinians just keeps exploding (figuratively).

And now she's old and has nothing to show for it. In America, most people retire at 65. Maybe Israel should start thinking about it too.

There's a Palestinian in the NFL!

July 16, 2013

Palestinian-Americans are split on a fundamental American issue: football. Many from my father's generation of immigrants are simply confused by the whole concept. They came from a land and time where "football" meant kicking a ball with your foot into a goal. Trying to divorce them from this word association is extremely difficult. The children of these immigrants, like me, who grew up in this country see football as the beautiful American tradition that it is. I have tried to explain to my father that a touchdown is basically a goal, and that each team is trying to get more touchdowns than the other. I told him it is "soccer with helmets," or "football with helmets," if, to you, "football" actually means "soccer."

But football is also a violent sport with fierce impacts, armor, and screaming. It brings men together in a passionate, non-sexual way. And it includes barely dressed women on the sidelines jumping up on down and sometimes even climbing on top of each other. Once my father learned these things, he became interested.

Oday Aboushi is a Palestinian-American. A few months ago, he was drafted by the New York Jets to play professional American football. I am sure this was a dream come true for him. Of course, we Palestinians all immediately heard the news. We have a secret e-mail list. We were proud. Most of us didn't know him, but we were proud.

Then last week, Yahoo! Sports published an article by Adam Waksman accusing Oday of "anti-Semitic activism." At just about the same time, an employee of Major League Baseball, Jonathan Mael tweeted, "The @nyjets are a disgrace of an organization. The Patriots have Aaron Hernandez, the Jets have Oday Aboushi." Of course, Aaron Hernandez is a star NFL tight end who has recently been arrested for murder. Oday is just a Palestinian.

Adjacent to Ramallah lies the city of El-Bireh in Palestine. Thousands of El-Bireh's descendants live in America. A couple weeks ago, they held a convention in a hotel outside of Washington, DC. It was basically a big family reunion. And I really mean that. When cousins start marrying each other,

109

family reunions need to be held in a hotel. A big hotel. But on the bright side, Ancestry.com loves Palestinian customers. Coming up with their report takes about five minutes. "Dear customer, your father is your mother's cousin. Your grandfathers are brothers, which also means they are each your great uncle. Your father is your father, but he is also your first cousin removed. Same goes for your mother. Your brothers and sisters are also each your second cousin. And you are also, in fact, your own cousin. Enjoy the rest of your day."

Oday Aboushi attended this convention as an invited guest. Waksman used his attendance as evidence of Oday's anti-Semitism. Oday was not quoted and none of his actions were detailed. He was just a guest at a big family reunion. See, to supporters of Israel like Mael and Waksman, and to many Jews unfortunately, Palestinians are by default anti-Semitic. But labeling us all as anti-Semitic is simply inaccurate. I can easily prove that I'm not an anti-Semite. I love bagels, cheesecake, and Seinfeld. And Jews invented the weekend, so those are my kind of people.

But using the "anti-Semitic" label so freely also does something else. It kills the conversation. Once someone is called a vicious racist, his opinion is less worthy. And so is his existence. And for Palestinians, we cannot end the conversation. We need to tell our story. So maybe those calling us "anti-Semitic" know exactly what they're doing.

Now I wouldn't mind being labeled, if only it were done accurately. Palestinian-Americans are some of the most successful and most educated citizens living in this country. We always do extremely well in whatever path we choose. Now, that might be because we don't have a country to go back to, but whatever. So none of us were surprised that Oday made all the way to the NFL. We expect excellence. Plus, for his own sake, he had to succeed. I don't even want to imagine what his mom would have done if he didn't get drafted.

Being Palestinian follows us wherever we go and whatever we do. Oday is now in the limelight. He will be seen as suspect. Fans will hold up signs. His existence will be highly politicized. Everything he does, good or bad, will have a lot of gravity to it. For every person praising him, there will be at least one other expressing outrage. He is a Palestinian, and so he will be seen as some sort of threat to the working order of things. And whether he likes it or not, his entry into the NFL will mean more than maybe it should. He is not a football player. He is a Palestinian football player.

110

Being Palestinian is unyielding. There are no breaks. And just when it looks like everything's OK, someone calls us "barbaric," "resentful," "hateful," or "invented." Our relatives who live in Palestine have to deal with daily killing and humiliation. Those of us who live everywhere else have to explain it.

Basically, Palestinians spend most of our time trying to explain to everyone that we are, in fact, human beings.

But don't feel bad for us. When we meet each other, we get excited. We share stories. We laugh and cry at the same things. When we say goodbye, we can't wait to see each other again. We have a connection to one another that no one else could ever understand.

And so Oday, when you were drafted, we were all drafted. And while my dad might not really understand football, he understands that.

Does Israel really care?

July 19, 2013

This week, there has been much talk about John Kerry's efforts to reignite the stalled peace process between the Israelis and the Palestinians. Kerry is confident, or so it seems, about the prospects of bringing everyone back together for fruitful talks.

Israel has put off negotiations for some time, opting to keep the status quo going. It is working out pretty well for her. The settlement building business is booming, Jerusalem is becoming less and less Arab, and all of it is happening with very little mention on the news.

The latest reports have stated that the Palestinians are telling Mr. Kerry that they will only come back to the table based on negotiations that would give a Palestinian state borders based on pre-1967 lines with minimal swaps. Israel has repeated her stance that she will not agree to any preconditions about discussions before discussing anything. Of course, that is just another way of saying that she doesn't want to negotiate anything at all.

Do you know why she doesn't want to negotiate anything? She doesn't care. Israel just doesn't care.

As a Palestinian, I think it's pretty cute that we really try to demand anything. We are powerless. Any form of statehood or independence is completely dependent on whether or not Israel wants to give it to us. And she doesn't care.

There need be no discussion on borders. If you ask a Palestinian to draw the borders of his country, he draws that familiar triangle that encompasses all of Israel, the West Bank, and Gaza Strip. That map is what we carry on our key chains. It is what we wear around our necks. It is what we know in our hearts.

If you ask an Israeli to draw his country, he draws the same thing. If you don't believe me, you can believe the Israeli Ministry of Tourism. The map of Israel it uses on its website does not show any borders at all around the West Bank. It even fully includes the occupied Golan Heights.

I'll tell you a secret. Even though we were kinda sorta expelled from our homes by Israel (even up until today), we're willing to share the whole thing. But Israel is not interested

112

in sharing of any kind. Do you know why? Because she just doesn't care.

There is no such thing as a "starting point" for negotiations when the party who holds all the cards is not interested in negotiating anything.

Israel continues to find ways to de-Palestinianize East Jerusalem. While building new neighborhoods and confiscating more land, Israel upholds laws meant to erase Palestinian existence there. Palestinians in East Jerusalem, although Israel annexed it long ago, are not citizens of Israel, but simply legal residents of the city. Families in which one parent holds Jerusalem residency and the other does not may not live together in the city. This leads to many families having to make the hard choice to leave Jerusalem, therefore running the risk of forever surrendering their Jerusalem residency.

Sounds inhumane and uncompassionate, right? But Israel doesn't care.

Israeli soldiers systematically dehumanize Palestinians and anyone who supports them. They have used Facebook to say every Palestinian child is a "little shit" and deserves a "bullet in his mouth." Just this week, reports surfaced that Israeli soldiers in training were making and eating "Rachel Corrie" pancakes. An Israeli bulldozer in Gaza flattened Rachel in 2003. Earlier this year, an Israeli solider posted an Instagram picture of a young Palestinian boy in the crosshairs of his rifle. How did Israel respond? She posted a YouTube video urging soldiers to use social media to show the "pretty face" of the IDF.

She really doesn't care.

Last month, a 100-year old Israeli general told the world that forces under his command destroyed Arab villages in 1948. He proudly said, "My conscience is at ease with that, because if we hadn't done so, then there would be no state by now. There would be a million more Arabs."

You don't really think she cares, do you?

Israel consistently tells us that she needs Palestinians to recognize her existence. Palestinians work in Israel, live under Israeli control, and use Israeli currency. We recognize Israel pretty strongly.

On the other hand, she still calls us a "demographic threat," destroys our villages whenever possible, and pretends our recipes belong to her. We don't need to recognize Israel, but maybe she should recognize us.

113

The starting point for dialogue is very simple. It is recognition of the truth. Palestinians can only feel comfortable speaking to Israel when she acknowledges the truth.

The time for denial is over.

Just say we were present.

Just say you kicked us out.

Just say you're still trying.

Just say falafel was here before you were.

Just say it. It will probably feel good.

And just say you're sorry. We don't care about anything else. Just that.

Any talks between us Palestinians and Israel must be preceded by just one thing: an unmitigated, unqualified, and genuine apology from her to us.

Before anything happens, we need to know that you think that we are actually human beings. We need to know that you actually care.

Then we can start talking.

There might be a ceremony, but so what?

So they tell us the Palestinians and Israelis are meeting in Jerusalem to discuss peace. There might be some papers signed, and there might even be a ceremony one day.

Now there are a lot of reasons to believe that these talks will lead nowhere. There is no real evidence that the Israelis are in any way interested in the Palestinians having any kind of state of their own. Settlement expansion in East Jerusalem and the West Bank is on the rise, and it is because the Israeli prime minister is pushing it. Let's be clear. Benjamin Netanyahu is not "giving in" to right-wing Israeli groups. He is their leader.

Now, we Palestinians might kick and scream a little bit, and we even pretended for a second that we wouldn't attend the negotiations. But of course we were going to attend. We don't have anything to lose at this point. Twenty years after the Oslo Accords, there is less of the West Bank to go toward a future state, and Palestinian rights are more marginalized than ever. Probably nothing will come of any negotiations, but at least the negotiators will get a hassle-free trip to Jerusalem, and trust me, those are hard to come by.

I have a feeling they are not really doing anything. I can only imagine what they are discussing:

Israeli Negotiator: Anyway, what do you want to do today?
Palestinian Negotiator: I think there is a 'Godfather' marathon on TV today.
Israeli: I'll make you an offer you can't refuse.
Palestinian: I'm not falling for that again... haha!
Israeli: Can't blame me for trying... Anyway, what time do you want to start 'negotiations' tomorrow?
Palestinian: I'm free anytime... Well, not really 'free,' if you know what I mean.

Of course, these negotiations are not going to produce any sort of long-lasting settlement. There might be some papers that get signed, and there might even be a ceremony. But I saw that twenty years ago too. I remember that day. I was 16

115

years old, and my history teacher actually took me out of class and let me watch the signing ceremony on live TV in the library. I was the only Palestinian in the school, and my parents were demonstration loving, well educated, and loud. In other words, they were Palestinian too. So my heritage was no secret in our white suburban community. When I played soccer as a child, my dad even insisted that my jersey number be "1948." "But baba, it's only supposed to be two digits," I pleaded. "Well, I was supposed to have a country, so we don't always get what we want." He had a point.

I sat and watched Clinton, Arafat, and Rabin stand on the White House Lawn. All I could remember thinking was, "Wow, Rabin and Arafat never looked that short on the news before." And I remember feeling conflicted. My parents were never in love with the PLO, and they were afraid that this agreement might be a disaster. But then again, there we were, on TV, shaking hands with the President of the United States of America. And who could say "no" to that? I mean, I watch Kim Kardashian on TV, and she seems like a self-centered, immoral, attention-grabbing woman who just makes one bad decision after another. But if she asked me out...

But back to today. Benjamin Netanyahu's entire tenure has been predicated on the idea that the Palestinians are not worthy of any rights whatsoever. He is a champion of settlements on Palestinian land. He has appointed ministers who are glorious anti-Arab racists. He makes coalitions with parties that believe the Palestinians have no rights in Israel, Jerusalem, or the West Bank. He refers to us pesky Palestinians as a "demographic threat."

We are less than human to the Israeli prime minister. One would imagine that, given his record, it would be foolish for America to think that he would allow any sort of real deal to occur. But the Americans know who Netanyahu is. They know he only sees Israel as existing in a Middle East where she must be in a constant state of war, ready to defend herself against an everlasting threat of annihilation by her neighbors. America allowing Benjamin Netanyahu to portray himself as someone who is even remotely interested in peace is perhaps the biggest insult of all.

Well, unlike the thinner and less-bald 16 year-old version of myself, I'm not conflicted about peace talks anymore. I know these are going nowhere, but the Israelis have shown up to them nonetheless, just to satisfy her patron. So Israel will talk, she might even sign some papers, and there might even be a ceremony. But just because your kid shows you a wet

116

toothbrush doesn't mean she actually brushed her teeth. You have to lean over and smell her breath.

20 years since Oslo

September 13, 2013

It's been 20 years since Oslo.

We Palestinians might not be good at everything, but we are strangely talented when it comes to knowing how long it has been since certain things happened.

It's been 65 years since the catastrophic events of 1948. Our land was ethnically cleansed. 400 Palestinian villages were destroyed. 750,000 registered refugees have now turned into 5 million.

It's been 46 years since the Six-Day War. 300,000 more refugees were created. 150,000 Palestinians became refugees for a second time. It was the beginning of military occupation, daily checkpoints, and constant curfews. Before 1967, over half of all Palestinians lived inside historic Palestine. After 1967, a vast majority did not.

It's been 106 years since the First Zionist Congress in Switzerland declared, "Zionism seeks to establish a home for the Jewish people in Palestine."

It's been 97 years since the Sykes-Picot Agreement. This is when snobby, aristocratic French and English men secretly agreed how they were going to carve up the Middle East after the Ottomans fell. Great Britain got Palestine.

It's been 96 years since the Balfour Declaration. Britain's Foreign Secretary expressed British support for a Jewish homeland in Palestine. To the Brits' credit, it was a very well mannered way of saying "we don't want you to live here in Europe."

It's been 26 years since the start of the First Intifada.

It's been 13 years since the start of the Second Intifada.

It's been 11 years since they started building the wall.

It's been 10 years since the murder of Rachel Corrie. She was the American-born activist killed when an American-made bulldozer crushed her as she non-violently protested the American-funded demolition of Palestinian homes in Gaza. Attempts to hold Israel accountable for this act have been unsuccessful. American governmental silence has been disgracefully deafening.

118

It's been 23 years since the massacre at al-Aqsa mosque in Jerusalem. 22 Palestinians were murdered in Jerusalem by Israeli security forces as they protested Israeli aggressions.

It's been 31 years since the massacres at Sabra and Shatila. Over 2,500 defenseless Palestinian refugees were murdered at the hands of Lebanese Phalangist forces in collaboration with Israel.

It's been 65 years since the massacre at Deir Yassin. Over 250 Palestinians were massacred, including at least 25 pregnant women.

It's been 5 years since the massacre in Gaza. 1,400 Palestinians were murdered indiscriminately in "Operation Cast Lead."

It's been 19 years since the massacre in Hebron. American-born Israeli Baruch Goldstein entered the Ibrahimi Mosque dressed in army fatigues and gunned down Palestinians as they knelt in worship. 29 were murdered and 125 were wounded. His gravesite became a site of pilgrimage for some Israelis.

It's been 60 years since the massacre at Qibya. 69 Palestinians were murdered in an operation ordered by David Ben-Gurion and commanded by Ariel Sharon. Sharon said, "Qibya was to be an example for everyone."

It's been 57 years since the massacres at Khan Yunis and Rafah. Over the course of eight days, almost 400 Palestinian refugees were massacred. Israel has never denied or acknowledging any wrongdoing.

It's been 57 years since the massacre at Kafr Qasem. 48 Palestinians were murdered by Israeli forces for violating a curfew they had no idea existed. Two soldiers were imprisoned for 5 years and later promoted to high-level positions inside Israel.

It's been 65 years since the massacres and expulsions in the Palestinian cities of Lidd and Ramle. Hundreds of Palestinians were murdered, scores of women were raped, and dozens of businesses were looted. 70,000 refugees were led, many on foot, to camps near Ramallah. Hundreds died on the way. Their empty houses were populated by Jewish immigrants who still reside there to this day.

You must be thinking, "Wow, that's a lot of massacres." One is a lot. This many... well, I don't know what that is.

It's been 65 years since my father was exiled from Palestine for being Palestinian, and 33 years since he was exiled from Jordan for the same reason.

119

And it's been 20 years since Oslo. I remember watching it on live TV. I was 16. I knew it was important, but I didn't quite know how to feel. Maybe there was something in my Palestinian DNA that told me that jubilation was not the proper response. Oslo, instead of being the end of a process (as many Palestinians incorrectly thought), was the beginning of a process. But it has not been a process of peace. It has been a process of expansion, settlements, dispossession, appropriation, and killing. It has been a process characterized by racist Israeli policies, right-wing Israeli politicians, and the denial of our very existence.

So, yes, it's been 20 years. But I don't really feel like talking about it. I have too many other things to remember.

Anthony Bourdain, will you marry me?

Something amazing happened on CNN last night. Palestinians were portrayed as human beings.

In his show "Parts Unknown," Anthony Bourdain travels to exotic and controversial locales to examine the intersection of food, politics, and everyday life. Last night, he visited Jerusalem, the West Bank, and Gaza.

He was immediately mesmerized by Palestine. That is a common phenomenon. It is an amazing place, where the gravity of the history and spirituality is heavy in the air. It feels majestic. But something is a little off. Bourdain felt the splendor, but, as he said, "Then you see the young draftees (teenage Israeli soldiers holding machine guns) in the streets, and you start to get the idea."

He began his journey with an Israeli chef and author, Yotam. They started by tasting some falafel in Jerusalem's Old City. Yotam told the audience, in a stunning admission, "Israelis made falafel their own, and everybody in the world thinks falafel is Israeli, but in actual fact, it is as much Palestinian, even more so, because it's been done for generations here... The question of food appropriation is massive here."

Now if they could only say the same thing about the land, the houses, and the air, we might be able to get somewhere.

Bourdain then made his way into the West Bank. And on his way to visit a settlement, he said something that Americans never hear on TV:

In 2003, Israel began construction on a wall along the green line representing the Israeli-Palestinian border. The wall now stretches 450 miles. When completed, it will span 700 miles, 85% of it in Palestinian territory... Since 1967, 500,000 Israeli settlers have moved into the West Bank, all in contravention of international law, many in contravention of Israeli law, though in effect it seems to make little difference, they're here and in ever larger numbers.

Anthony, you will be hearing from certain individuals and organizations in the coming days. They will be upset. They've been trying to keep this stuff a secret.

121

Before he arrived to the settlement, he noticed some Hebrew graffiti on a Palestinian house in a neighboring village. His driver translated it for him: "Death to Arabs."

Anthony, you will be hearing from certain individuals and organizations in the coming days. They will be upset. They've been trying to keep this stuff a secret.

Bourdain finally made it to the settlement of Eli. Eli is located north of Ramallah and in the heart of the West Bank. It is nowhere near the 1967 borders. He asked its chief executive, Amiad, what Palestinians might think of its existence. He told Bourdain, "Actually they are happy we are here. We gave them prosperity for the past 45 years." I was worried the show might go in a bad direction, but then Bourdain said, "I'm guessing a lot of people would disagree with that statement." Wow, I think he's getting it. Then Bourdain said, "So, from the high ground, you can see anyone walking at night, you can see pretty far out." Wow, he is getting it!

Anthony, you will be hearing from certain individuals and organizations in the coming days. They will be upset. They've been trying to keep this stuff a secret.

As Bourdain prepared to leave Eli, he brought up with Amiad the disturbing graffiti he saw. "Why not paint it over?" he asked innocently. The response? "Good question. Maybe we should. You're right." I'm sure Anthony knows he's not the first person to suggest such a thing. Now, Anthony, I am a bit more experienced with Israeli talk than you are, so let me translate that. "Good question. Maybe we should. You're right," really means, "Silly question, we definitely won't, get out of my face."

Bourdain then made a quick visit with a now famous group of female Palestinian thrill-seeking drivers called "The Speed Sisters." Now this visit had nothing to do with food, but he was able to be in a car alone with a hot Palestinian woman. And you don't turn down an opportunity like that. He even looked like he caught a little case of Palestinian fever. I can relate.

After visiting Jerusalem, Bourdain took the short but interesting drive into Bethlehem, through a checkpoint, and past the infamous wall:

> It's right there for all to see. And it feels like something out of a science fiction film. This is the wall. From the other side, from inside this place, it doesn't feel like anything other than what it is: a prison.

122

Anthony, you will be hearing from certain individuals and organizations in the coming days. They will be upset. They've been trying to keep this stuff a secret.

Bourdain visited Aida refugee camp, just north of Bethlehem. There he met Abdelfattah Abusrour, my friend, and the founder of Ruwwad, a group that uses theatre for young people to air their desires and feelings. Abusrour sees Ruwwad as nonviolent resistance, a way for young people to express themselves, creating what he calls "a peace from within."

The honest portrayal of the residents of the camp, from their squalor to their own struggle to find productive channels of resistance, was something I had never seen on American TV. Bourdain noted that these Palestinian children do not have the luxury of idolizing pop stars and athletes. They turn to politics early, sometimes idolizing martyrs and politicians. And he's right, there's something wrong with that. We Palestinians are normal in so many ways. And we're so not normal in so many others.

Then Bourdain went to Gaza:

Getting in and out of Gaza from Israel is truly one of the most surreal travel experiences you could have on Earth. Over 1.5 million people live in Gaza, most of them considered refugees, meaning they are not from the place they are compelled to live now. In most cases, they are either prohibited from or unable to leave. Israel decides who comes and goes, what gets in and what stays out.

Anthony, you will be hearing from certain individuals and organizations in the coming days. They will be upset. They've been trying to keep this stuff a secret.

In Gaza, he met Laila Haddad, a well-known Palestinian author and activist who has written books about Gaza life and cuisine. As she explained that Gaza's fare should include a lot of seafood, she noted that fishermen could rarely get prize catches as the Israeli military limits how far out they can sail. If they go too far, the Israeli navy shoots at their boats and cuts their nets.

Bourdain and Haddad then visited the Sultan family, where they were served a Palestinian staple, maqloobeh. That dish happens to be one of my specialties (Yes, ladies, I can cook). As they were eating, the man of the house was worried about being rude. Why? The cameramen were not eating. His wife asked Bourdain to open a restaurant for her in America. We Palestinians are always looking for a hook-up. We need it.

123

Her husband continued to yell, but Leila assured Anthony, "This is a normal tone of voice. He's not upset, by the way. This is how we talk. We yell." I can definitely relate.

Before Bourdain left Gaza, he met and dined with one more group of men. These men, like 75% of Gaza's population, were refugees. As he sat, laughing and eating, he told us:

> *Many of these guys are not too sympathetic to my country, or my ethnicity I'm guessing. But, there's that hospitality thing. Anywhere you go in the Muslim world, it seems, no matter what, you feed your guests, you do your best to make them feel at home.*

It's true. We Palestinians are overly hospitable when people visit our homeland. Sometimes too much.

The episode ended with Natan, the owner of a restaurant right outside of Gaza in Israel. Natan's daughter was killed by a mortar bomb in the constant struggle between groups in Gaza and Israel. Since 2008, over 1,600 Palestinians in Gaza have also been killed in this conflict.

Natan spoke of the senseless deaths on both sides. He clearly disliked settlements, and he believed it was possible for like-minded people from both sides to get together and make peace. I would agree, if just more people like Natan existed. But the people pointing the guns at me aren't named Natan... They're named Netanyahu.

By the end, Bourdain did not seem too optimistic about the prospects of peace. "One doesn't even have to speak metaphorically because there is an actual wall... or a fence, depending on who you're talking to." Natan told him, "No. It is a big wall. It is ugly. It is really ugly. You can see it, it's not far away from here." Unfortunately, it's not far away from anywhere.

Anthony, you will be hearing from certain individuals and organizations in the coming days. They will be upset. They've been trying to keep this stuff a secret.

Part of being Palestinian in America is getting really excited whenever someone tells the truth about us on American TV. Kind of depressing, right?

Anthony, in the beginning of this episode, you gave the following disclaimer:

> *By the end of this hour, I'll be seen by many as a terrorist sympathizer, a Zionist tool, a self-hating Jew, an apologist for American imperialism, an Orientalist, socialist, a fascist, CIA agent, and worse.*

I didn't see any of that. I just saw what happens to anyone who actually interacts with Palestinians. You fell in love with us, and we fell in love with you.

Bibi Netanyahu's Twilight Zone

October 2, 2013

It's hard to describe what it felt like listening to Benjamin Netanyahu speak yesterday at the United Nations. Many phrases came to mind: "alternative reality," "parallel universe," "clinical denial," and the list goes on. Then I remembered one of my favorite TV shows that I used to watch as a kid:

You are about to enter another dimension. A dimension not only of sight and sound, but of mind. A journey into a wondrous land of imagination. Next stop, the Twilight Zone!

Netanyahu introduced himself:

I feel deeply honored and privileged to stand here before you today representing the citizens of the state of Israel. We are an ancient people. We date back nearly 4,000 years to Abraham, Isaac and Jacob. We have journeyed through time. We've overcome the greatest of adversities. And we reestablished our sovereign state in our ancestral homeland, the land of Israel.

Of course, 1.2 million of Israel's citizens are Palestinians. That means about 20% of Israelis are non-Jews. Benjamin Netanyahu made it clear that he does not speak for them. We Palestinians kind of already knew that.

In America, about 13% of the population is black. In today's world, we cannot imagine an American president, even a white one, explicitly stating that he does not include them in his ranks.

But to Netanyahu, these 1.2 million people do not exist. If that's not living in another dimension, I don't know what is.

He then started talking about Iran. And he kept talking about Iran. And kept talking. In fact, he spent 2535 of his 3015 words talking about Iran. I counted. That's 84%. Iranian president Hassan Rouhani didn't even spend 84% of his time talking about Iran.

He then went into the background of Hassan Rouhani. We learned that Rouhani was a member of Iran's national security council for some time. We also learned that he was Iran's chief nuclear negotiator for a couple years and has been involved in Iran's government at different levels for a really long time. I didn't know any of that. Who needs Wikipedia when we have Bibi?

Rouhani is worse than Ahmadinejad, he says, because as his predecessor was a "wolf in wolf's clothing," Rouhani is a "wolf in sheep's clothing." One can see Bibi's point here. If you remember, Ahmadinejad's beard was dark and scraggly. Rouhani's is white and lush. Ahmadinejad did look more like a wolf, and Rouhani definitely looks more like a sheep.

Rouhani, according to Netanyahu, is cold, calculating, and deceptive. We, the international community, would be making a huge mistake by trusting him. Bibi backs up his argument by telling us that one of Rouhani's devious tactics is to "smile a lot." Is he telling us that smiling Muslims can't be trusted? In that case, I guess I should look at everything my grandfather ever told me with a little more suspicion. Or is it just that smiling Iranians can't be trusted? In that case, no more Maz Jobrani shows for me. Or maybe he means that smiling politicians can't be trusted. In that case, we can definitely trust Bibi. He never smiles.

I'm sure Netanyahu has never met a smiling Muslim. It's hard to smile with a M-16 in your face.

Netanyahu went on to detail how Iran is building a nuclear weapon. He talked of warheads, percentages of uranium enrichment, stockpiles, and intercontinental ballistic missiles. In fact, according to him, Iran will soon have missiles that could reach New York City. And they're doing all of this in secret. Scary stuff indeed.

Actually, Netanyahu speaks from some authority on this subject. If anyone knows how to build a secret nuclear weapons program, it's Israel. Israel has had a stated policy of "nuclear ambiguity" for over 50 years. That means no admissions, no inspections, and no accounting. In fact, despite international calls, Israel has never signed nor ratified the Nuclear Non-Proliferation Treaty.

In his speech to the General Assembly, Netanyahu said, "facts are stubborn things." Israel has at least 200 nuclear warheads. They even have those scary intercontinental ballistic missile things Bibi warned us about. But in Israel's alternate dimension of existence, everyone should follow the rules, except her. Stubborn indeed.

Rouhani has stated that Iran's nuclear program is peaceful. He even told American news outlets that Iran would never seek to build weapons of mass destruction. But this is not enough for Israel's prime minister. It's almost as if Netanyahu doesn't know how to live in a world where Iran does not want to obliterate Israel from the face of the earth.

Now I guess no one really knows for sure whether or not Iran actually wishes to develop nuclear weapons capabilities. Maybe they're trying. But Netanyahu asked, "Why does Rouhani think that he can get away with it?" Well, he doesn't need to look far... just about 3 countries to the west.

Then Benjamin Netanyahu did something that might have been worse than any of the human rights violations that Israel has ever committed. After describing how the new Iranian president was duping us all, he said, "Rouhani thinks he can have his yellowcake and eat it too." Oy vey, Bibi. I know there is a long tradition of Jewish comedians. But please, for God's sake, leave the jokes to us professionals.

And if you still don't believe that Netanyahu lives in a world of "wondrous imagination," you only had to listen to how he scolded anyone who might take Rouhani at his word:

The last century has taught us that when a radical regime with global ambitions gets awesome power, sooner or later its appetite for aggression knows no bounds.

Tell me about it.

Of course, he addressed the Palestinian question briefly. He said he wanted to have successful negotiations where a new Palestinian state would be demilitarized. This is kind of like saying a wife wants to have successful negotiations with her husband about how often they should go curtain shopping. Problem: he doesn't want to go curtain shopping.

But just when I didn't think Benjamin Netanyahu could sound any more cuckoo, he outdid himself:

In our time the Biblical prophecies are being realized. As the prophet Amos said, they shall rebuild ruined cities and inhabit them. They shall plant vineyards and drink their wine. They shall till gardens and eat their fruit.

Now, in the real world, you don't get credit for rebuilding ruined cities if you're the one who devastated and emptied them, stealing their vineyards and looting their gardens along the way. But in Netanyahu's alternative universe, these stubborn facts don't exist.

We all loved "The Twilight Zone." It was beautifully imaginative and entertaining. But after watching each episode, we were always mindful of one thing: It was all a fantasy.

128

Palestinian talking points

October 30, 2013

Last weekend, college students from around the country converged on Stanford University for a conference of the Students for Justice in Palestine. SJP representatives from dozens of universities got together to discuss strategies, experiences, and proposals. I remember attending and organizing conferences like these when I was a student at the University of Michigan, and if these students were anything like me, they must have been exhilarated.

In my days as a student, I participated in and led dozens of demonstrations. We created mock checkpoints, we brought in speakers, and we even blindfolded ourselves and pretended we were prisoners once. Pretending is much better than the real thing.

I'm sure their most recent gathering energized this new batch of students. But I thought I might help out a little bit with some Palestinian talking points for anyone interested.

I'll just suggest answers to some of the most common arguments posed by pro-Israeli groups. Before I begin, it is important to understand that most of the individuals who make these pro-Israel arguments live in an alternate reality. Therefore, if they do not respond well to the counterarguments that I suggest, you should not take it personally. Feeling sorry for them would probably be more appropriate.

Israel has already made painful concessions by withdrawing from Gaza and Lebanon.

No. Withdrawing from land you gained and occupied illegally through force is not a "concession." "Concession" comes from the verb "concede." To "concede" means to "admit that something is true or valid after first denying or resisting it." So, for instance, one might accurately say, "Israel recently made a painful concession by stating that hummus is, in fact, part of native Palestinian cuisine and has absolutely nothing to do with Israeli culture." I can dream, can't I?

Dismantling unjust and unlawful conditions that you created in the first place is not a "concession." If you think it is, you might be living in an alternate universe. You may also

129

still be wondering why Santa Claus never responded to any of your letters.

Israel is the only democracy in the Middle East.

Nope. This one is especially delusional. Let's first assume, for the sake of argument, that Israel is a "democracy." If she were, would she be the "only" one? "Only" is defined as "being the single one," or "single in distinction." Of course, we now have democracies in Iraq, Tunisia, and Egypt. Egyptians are so democratic that they demonstrated against Mubarak, and then ousted Mubarak, and then elected Morsi, and then demonstrated against Morsi, and then ousted Morsi. That is democracy in full force.

Lebanon is sort of democratic, and Iran has democratic tendencies too. In fact, until a few years ago, Lebanon and Iran were the only other countries in the Middle East to have something called a "living former president." If that's not a sign of democracy, I don't know what it is.

But, of course, the real question we should ask ourselves is whether or not Israel actually is a "democracy." "Democracy" means "government by the people, where the supreme power is vested in the people and exercised directly by them or by their elected agents under a free electoral system." It could also mean "a state of society characterized by formal equality of rights and privileges."

Israel operates two separate school systems for its almost 2 million schoolchildren. One is for Jewish students, and one is for Arab students. Israel spends about $1 on Arab students for every $3 it spends on Jewish students. That doesn't sound like "formal equality." Palestinians are denied adequate resources and their identity is completely ignored in the teaching process.

About half of Israel's Palestinian college graduates are jobless. The infant mortality rate among Arab citizens of Israel is two and a half times that of Jews. Arab elementary and middle school students trail their Jewish counterparts in math, science, and English, and the gap is widening. Remember, sixty years ago, when America decided that "separate but equal" was an illusion? Well, Israel never got the memo.

Sure, Israel's Palestinian citizenry of about 1.5 million people can vote. But the ability to vote is not the only measure of a democracy. If you go to the gym once a week, are you healthy? If you go to the gym every day but still eat fried food for breakfast, lunch and dinner, are you healthy? If you spend

130

45 minutes a day on the treadmill but still end each evening with your favorite hookah, are you healthy? Democracy is not about occasional practices here and there. It's about continuously working hard in every way to maintain that sexy figure. It is about a state of mind.

If you think Israel is a functioning democracy that cares about all of its citizens, you may be hallucinating and hearing voices. I would suggest therapy, followed by an aggressive regimen of antipsychotic medications.

Israel and America have shared values.

No. I was an American student. I grew up in American history, government, and social studies classes. And there was one thing that was constantly drilled into our brains. "We, the People of the United States, in Order to form a more perfect Union..." That's right, the Constitution. It is at the heart, implicitly or explicitly, of every political and legal discussion in this country. It denotes our individual rights, and it enshrines our political and social values. Our politicians take an oath to uphold it. Our civil rights movements would have gotten nowhere without it. It is the heartbeat of our democracy.

In fact, we value constitutions so much that when we invaded Iraq, toppled Saddam, and rebuilt their government, the first thing we did was to help them write a new constitution. We spent millions of dollars and lent them some of our most prominent legal scholars. The Iraqi constitution has numerous provisions guaranteeing civil rights, political rights, and personal liberty. It even codifies the principle that all people are equal before the law, regardless of religion or ethnicity.

In the Israeli constitution... oh yeah, Israel has no constitution. And there is a simple reason for that. Israel does not want to codify into a sacred document what she truly believes: the only people who should receive the full protection of the government and its laws are Jews and Jews only. Creating a constitution would either force Israel to join the civilized world and declare all of her citizens as equals or oblige her to actually engrave her discriminatory beliefs onto tablets of stone for all of humanity to see. But why make that choice when you don't have to?

Israel and America might share bank accounts, but they don't share values. If you think they do, you might suffer from pseudologia fantastica, or pathological lying. There are support groups for that.

131

Israel is not an apartheid state like South Africa was.

Well, this one is actually true. "Apartheid" in South Africa was an official policy of segregation or discrimination on grounds of race. Remember, Israel has no constitution. And she really has no "official policies." She simply chooses to pretend as if Jews are the only people living under her control.

See, apartheid in South Africa was very ugly, but at least it was clear. When white Afrikaners established apartheid rule in 1948 (coincidence?), it was unique from segregation anywhere else in that it was actually formalized through national law. The South African government was unabashedly honest in its racism. Sure, Israel has separate roads and buses for Jews and Palestinians, military checkpoints, discriminatory marriage laws, Jewish-only settlements, and a big, ugly wall. We Palestinians, like the black South Africans under apartheid rule, are being treated as subhuman by the government that rules over us. There can be no arguing that.

But the weird thing about apartheid is that in order to practice it you must announce that you are practicing it. David Ben-Gurion once said that unless Israel was successful in ridding itself of the Arabs, it would become an apartheid state. What he meant was that a government based on ethnic or racial superiority in a land with more than one ethnicity or race can only masquerade as a democracy for so long. Eventually, you need to either get rid of the other races or actually make laws to preserve your own superiority.

Israel is not an apartheid state. Not yet. But she is definitely on her way.

There are many more Israeli arguments to be counter-argued with truth and logic. If I can be of any further assistance, get in touch with me. I'm a comedian, so I am usually free on... well, I'm always free.

Mandela and my daily Palestinian moment

December 8, 2013

I wasn't going to write anything in the wake of the death of Nelson Mandela. I thought it would be lost in the sea of posts and columns praising the man as a revolutionary figure for freedom.

I expected to see numerous news outlets, politicians, and commentators sanitize him, turning him into some sort of conciliatory figure that we could all universally digest. I didn't expect much review of the history of apartheid in South Africa or Mandela's radical history in uprooting it.

I was watching CNN on Friday, the day after his death was announced. Much of the coverage revolved around Mandela and world reactions to his death. The stories were varied:

Mandela Memorial
Ex-Fellow Inmate Remembers Mandela
How Mandela Influenced Obama
Crowds Gather to Mourn Mandela
Mandela to Lie in State Next Week

It was everything I expected to see. And just as I was about to turn off the TV and get on with the rest of my day, my daily Palestinian moment happened. Sometime in the early afternoon, Wolf Blitzer popped on to the screen with none other than former Israeli prime minister, defense minister, and commando Ehud Barak. Now I couldn't turn off the TV. My "Palestinianality" required me to watch.

I imagine that Mr. Barak's appearance on CNN that day was scheduled well before the news of Mandela's death broke. But who cares? What happened next is the really interesting part. Blitzer quickly noted that Mandela had criticized Israel in the past and then asked Barak to describe his thoughts when the former president of South Africa visited the former prime minister of Israel:

I was a young prime minister... He tried to convince us that we should do more... He had very clear ideas. I tried to convince him somehow Arafat is not of the same character in

133

terms in greatness and a much more kind of narrow, fixated kind of character. But he, you know, he supported the idea. He felt that there are certain similarities, however remote, with that situation and tried very hard to convince us that nothing which seems now to be an obstacle should not be taken as an insurmountable because when there is a will, we can overcome everything.

Nelson Mandela is one of the greatest statesmen of the 20th century. He left imprints on hundreds of millions, not just on his own people, and changed history as a result of being consistent, determined, in a way, a benign zealot. He was zealot for his case but a great kind of mind and open-minded, could carry the burden of not just the responsibility to lead but also responsibility to be self-disciplined once he won.

That is what he said according to CNN. I know that some of it sounds incoherent. But in all fairness, English is, at best, Barak's second language. And since I consistently deal with people for whom English is a second, third, or fourth language, I can sympathize.

But a couple of things were clear from Barak's words.

First, he reminded us all that Arafat was no Mandela. This is undeniably true. Mandela understood that he must be un-wavering until the full measure of justice was dispensed. He knew that he could not allow his oppressors to shake his hand on a world stage, using him to pretend that everything was all right. He understood that he could not share a Nobel Peace Prize with his counterpart until the racist system that had for so long tormented his homeland was completely done away with. He would have never signed the Oslo Accords. He rec-ognized that justice could not be delivered piecemeal, morsel by morsel. He understood all of these things. Arafat did not.

So, yes, Arafat was no Mandela. But the absence of a Pales-tinian Mandela is no excuse for the continued Israeli treat-ment of us as subhuman. Unless, of course, you are Ehud Barak or just about every other Israeli leader. In their world, Palestinians must behave before any sort of Israeli "conces-sions" can take place. Additionally, in their world, Palestini-ans never behave. Since Palestinians never behave, Israel cannot make any "concessions." Do you understand? It is very important to understand this way of Israeli thinking. Other-wise, Ehud Barak's statements might seem like complete nonsense.

Second, his praise for Mandela was muted, calling him a "benign zealot." Now I will be the first to say that I have heard this term before, but I am not always sure exactly what it means. A "zealot," by definition, is "a person who is fanatical and uncompromising in pursuit of his religious, political, or other ideals." "Benign" can mean "gentle" or "agreeable." It can also mean "harmless." Now, if Barak meant that Mandela was a nice guy, it seems from everything that I have ever seen that he is correct. But that is not what he meant. "Benign zealot" is a term used by oppressors to describe the kind of zealots they are willing to live with.

Of course, Mandela was not "benign" in any sense of the word. One can very strongly make the case that without him, apartheid in South Africa may not have been abolished, or at least not as quickly. He was not "harmless," at least not as far as the South African regime of that time was concerned. One could also say, almost without any doubt at all, that Nelson Mandela would have never have described himself as a "benign zealot." But this is of no concern to Ehud Barak. In his world, Mandela became acceptable only when he became "benign." A gentle former revolutionary in post-apartheid South Africa could visit Israel in 1999. Of course, just ten years earlier, Israel, along with Ronald Reagan, had supported the apartheid regime. In fact, immediately after his release in 1990, almost every country in the world invited Mandela to visit. Israel did not.

I am writing all of these things because it is important to understand this type of Israeli thinking. Otherwise, Ehud Barak's statements might seem like complete nonsense.

After Mandela's death, Israeli President Shimon Peres got in on the praising as well, calling Mandela a "venerable leader" and a "strong proponent of democracy." Netanyahu joined in, describing Mandela as a "freedom fighter who opposed violence" and a "man of vision."

Now, perhaps you can imagine the sense of ironic disbelief and paradoxical astonishment I experienced in these "Palestinian moments" listening to Barak, Peres, and Netanyahu. If you cannot, let me try to make an analogy.

Listening to Israeli prime ministers praise Nelson Mandela is as ridiculous as...well, it's as ridiculous as listening to Israeli prime ministers praise Nelson Mandela. Sorry, that's the best I can do.

The Failure of Israel

January 14, 2014

It is time. It is time to talk about the failure of Israel. I am not speaking of a singular or minor failure here and there. I am talking about the failure of the whole enterprise. Reports are trickling out that the secret Palestinian-Israeli peace negotiations are in trouble. This should come as no surprise. Israel doesn't really want to negotiate, and the Palestinians have nothing to negotiate with.

But why do I say Israel is a failure? How could I say such a thing? Hasn't she created a vibrant society in the middle of conflict, tension, and despair? Hasn't she built institutions and industries that are to be envied? Hasn't she established a first-world economy and civilization in a sea of third-world backwards peoples that wouldn't know modernity if it slapped them in the face?

All of those things are true. But it doesn't matter. Israel is still a failure.

Wearing fancy clothes, driving luxury cars, and having a fat wallet don't necessarily mean that you're more successful than everyone else around you. Those things don't make you smarter. Look at Paris Hilton. They don't make you kinder. Look at Rupert Murdoch. And they don't even make you better looking. Look at Donald Trump... but not for too long.

So, what are the elements of Israel's failure? Let's break it down.

Israel has a bad relationship with every single one of her neighbors.

Egypt, Jordan, Syria, and Lebanon all border Israel. And while peace agreements with Egypt and Jordan have been signed, they were done so with little public support and are, by their nature, fragile. And we don't even have to talk about Israel's rapport with Syria and Lebanon. Syria is Israel's go-to enemy, as she seeks every reason to demonize Syria and Syrians at every turn. Oh, and Israel illegally occupies 500 square miles of Syrian land in the Golan Heights. That's 15 Manhattans. Then, when it comes to Lebanon, Israel, like clockwork, orchestrates a bombing campaign there every few years or so.

136

If it's time for the Olympics, Israel is probably bombing Lebanon.

Israel subjects 5 million people to a military occupation.

The illegal Israeli military occupation of the West Bank and Gaza has been in place since 1967. It is shameful, violent, and unlawful. It imperils not only those living under it, but also the entirety of the Israeli population. It treats Palestinians as subhuman, requiring them to travel through their own land as if they don't belong. It consistently perpetrates unspeakable violence against its imprisoned and impoverished inhabitants, via both highly trained, heavily equipped soldiers and armed, unaccountable, ideological settlers. Moreover, the occupation is expensive, costing Israel something to the tune of $5 billion a year. Highly developed democratic nations don't go around occupying populations that rival their own in number.

Israel cannot exist without violence.

Almost all the talk from Israeli politicians revolves around war and aggression. Almost none of it focuses on the ills of that bad habit. "If America doesn't take out Iran, then we will! If America doesn't take out Syria, then we will! If America doesn't take out 'The Real Housewives of New Jersey,' then we will!"

Last week, Ariel Sharon was finally pronounced dead. To Palestinians, his image was that of a mass murderer. But I am not here to rehash Sharon's legacy. But it is important to note that his people deemed him "indirectly responsible" for the massacre of 2,500 Palestinians in the refugee camps of Sabra and Shatila in 1982. (By the way, for those of you who don't speak "Israeli," I can tell you that "indirectly responsible" actually means "definitely 100% responsible.") Those same people later awarded him with four ministries and eventually elected him prime minister from 2001-2006. Frankly, I am much less concerned with Sharon than I am with the society that knew exactly who he was and celebrated him nonetheless. Many say Israel is accustomed to war. Perhaps the truth is that she is addicted to it.

Israel is almost completely dependent on the United States.

According to Israeli news sources, US aid to Israel has totaled over $233 billion since 1949. This works out to almost $5 billion a year (remember the cost of the occupation above?).

Aside from the financial aid, Israel depends on American political cover in the international community. Since 1972, America has vetoed at least 42 United Nations Security Council Resolutions critical of Israel. Among these were resolutions demanding Israel cease construction of settlements in east Jerusalem, confirming Israeli expropriation of land in east Jerusalem as invalid, urging Israel to abide by the Fourth Geneva Convention, condemning Israeli actions against civilians in southern Lebanon, calling on Israel to withdraw from all Palestinian territories, and 3 separate resolutions asking Israel to halt military operations in Gaza. With all this reliance on the United States, can we really call Israel a success?

Israel hasn't achieved it most important and vital goal.

Since 1948, Israel has had one fundamental objective: To rid herself of the Palestinians. To her credit, she has tried, energetically, vigorously, forcefully, and robustly. But her efforts have borne no fruit. We exist today just as vociferously and enthusiastically as we ever have. It must be understood that by the nature of Israel's ideology, the eradication of any sign of the Palestinians is crucial to her success. She wants us to be permanently out of commission. She does, however, want to keep the hummus and the hookahs.

Israel doesn't know what else to do.

This is the most important element of Israel's failure. War has failed. Expulsions have failed. Settlements have failed. Massacres have failed. It's time for some new strategies. The only thing Israel hasn't tried is collective democracy (not Jewish-only democracy) and the recognition of universal human rights. One wonders if she is capable of such a thing.

Last week, according to Haaretz, Netanyahu told his fellow party members that he is against evacuating settlements like Hebron and Beit El. He called them "important to the Jewish people." Beit El houses about 6,000 mostly Orthodox settlers and sits adjacent to the twin cities of Ramallah and El-Bireh, which together contain about 80,000 Palestinians. The population of Hebron numbers about 250,000 Palestinians and 600 ideological Jewish settlers. Netanyahu is basically talking about keeping settlements that are outside the major settlement blocs but have military and ideological importance. This is the "same old same old," and it has never worked before.

138

Even the dumbest guy starts using different pickup lines up-on rejection after rejection.

"He also said he has 'no solution' for how to prevent Israel from becoming a binational state while also ensuring that a Palestinian state won't become a base for Iran or Al-Qaeda." A couple of things are clear here. First, Netanyahu obviously views a binational state as a disaster. There is no surprise here, as he has been known to call us Palestinians a "demo-graphic threat," which, by the way Bibi, hurts our feelings. Second, he believes we crazy Palestinians would be open to either Iran or Al-Qaeda, which, by the way Bibi, are ideologi-cal opposites and hate each other. And we wouldn't be open to either of them in any case. While we are usually welcoming, we now know that it is generally a bad idea to open our homes to someone without knowing his true intentions. We learned that lesson 65 years ago.

Netanyahu also described his general position on us pesky natives. "There's a problem that the Palestinians are there, and I have no intention of removing them. It's impractical and inappropriate." Inappropriate? Pretty callous. Bibi then de-scribed slavery as "impolite" and apartheid as "inconsiderate."

Netanyahu concluded his meeting: "Currently, we have no solution."

For the longest time, we Palestinians have been telling our-selves, "Look, how smart Israeli is! She plans a hundred years into the future!" Well, it turns out that we were all wrong. Israel only looks as far as the next Palestinian.

Israel is not a success in any real sense of the word. She is cruel, militaristic, aggressive, and needy. She deflects criti-cism and flouts international values. She even built a wall. She can currently be found banging her head against it.

A Letter to Israel from a sympathetic Palestinian

February 16, 2014

Dear Israel,

I know how you feel.

It's been a tough year. And it's only just started. Your world seems like it's crumbling around you. Everything you knew is no longer true. The comfortable circumstances to which you have become accustomed are rapidly changing around you. And worse yet, it seems you can do nothing about it.

I know how you feel.

Your so-called "friends" are turning on you. They said they would all always stand by you, no matter what. And now, just when it seems that you need them the most, they have forsaken you.

I know how you feel.

About a month ago, I attended a lecture in Ann Arbor, Michigan by one of the leaders of the boycott, divestment, and sanctions movement (BDS). After the speaker completed his presentation, many audience members approached the microphones to ask questions, continuing the discussion. Among the many participants were a few pro-Israel attendees who challenged the speaker on his assertions and arguments. As I sat there watching them, I remembered how, many years ago, I used to attend events sponsored by pro-Israel groups on that same campus. They would invite ambassadors, generals, and academics to argue for you. A few other interested Palestinians and I would stride in that hostile sea, and we would plead our case. We would wonder if anyone was really listening. We would doubt that anyone would ever see the world the way we do. We would sit there, looking around, feeling alone, as if no one understood us, and as if no one ever would. When I saw those students standing up for you last month, they had the same dejected look on their faces I bore over fifteen years ago. It must have felt terrible.

So, I know how you feel.

The position you currently find yourself in is full of uncertainty, discomfort, and doubt. It is as if no matter what you do or say, you just can't get anyone to believe you. You don't know where to turn. You can't figure out what to do. You're lost. Was everything you've ever told yourself just one big lie? Were you going about things the wrong way this whole time? You're wondering, fearful and apprehensive, about what the future holds. You're thinking, "What am I going to do now?"

At one time or another, I have asked myself all those same questions. Trust me, more anger is not the answer. I've tried it, and it just doesn't work. Change is hard. But having everything you've ever known uprooted is not a death sentence. I got through it, and so can you.

Trust me, I know how you feel.

Recently, your days have been full of turmoil and os. The past several months for you have been bad. Really bad. But you've only had a bad few months. I've had a bad 65 years. I know I'm only 36, but I was born in 1948, just like the rest of us.

So you'll survive. I promise. You just have to accept the fact that things are never going to be the same.

While I can sympathize, there is one major difference. Like you, I have always felt that the truth was on my side. But unlike you, it turns out that I was right.

Nevertheless, I'm here for you. And I promise you, I'm not going anywhere. We'll get through this.

Sincerely,
A Sympathetic Palestinian

141

Abbas, returning the Right of Return

February 23, 2014

Last week, the Palestinian right of return made a special news appearance. For some time, the issue has been a sticking point in negotiations between Israel and the Palestinians. Refusal to budge on the right has been the cornerstone of any Palestinian position. Refusal to recognize it has been at the heart of any Israeli policy. Since 1993, it has been perhaps the most contentious issue, the one on which Palestinians and Israelis, even in their respective publics, are diametrically opposed. It was one of the few things we could actually agree to never agree upon. That symmetric status quo was where we always found ourselves. Until this week.

But before I get to the somewhat controversial words of the Palestinian president Mahmoud Abbas, let me briefly outline where the right of return comes from.

The Universal Declaration of Human Rights, adopted by all United Nations member states on December 10, 1948, including Israel, states, "Everyone has the right to leave any country, including his own, and to return to his country." General Assembly Resolution 194, passed by the UN the very next day, read that Palestinian refugees wishing to return to their homes should be able to do so, adding that those who did not should be compensated justly. Following the 1967 Six-Day War, the UN Security Council passed Resolution 242, affirming the necessity for "achieving a just settlement of the refugee problem." In 1974, following a speech by Yasser Arafat, the UN General Assembly passed Resolution 3236, which "reaffirms also the inalienable right of the Palestinians to return to their homes and property from which they have been displaced and uprooted, and calls for their return." Finally, the International Covenant on Civil and Political Rights, ratified by Israel in 1991, states, "No one shall be arbitrarily deprived of the right to enter his own country."

Wow, that's a lot of international law and declarations. One would imagine that Israel, with her wealth of great legal minds and allies, must have a well thought out, deliberate, and logical response to all of that. Well, one should not hope too enthusiastically. Israel's response is, basically, "Well, re-

142

gardless of all of that legal stuff, we just don't wanna do it. It would kind of mess up what we've built over here."

See, we Palestinians have gotten pretty tired of complaining about how international law should be protecting us. As long as the Israelis live in an alternate reality, such logical arguments don't get us very far.

Israel has summarily disregarded any sort of rights for Palestinian refugees since 1948. She has even gone as far as to create bizarre conditions, disallowing Palestinian citizens of Israel to reclaim their properties, even if they were only gone for a short time during the events of 1948, even if they could prove ownership, and even if they still live right down the street. Israel said these persons were "absent." Then these persons showed up shortly after being expelled from their homes, thus making them "present." Israel then gave them the befuddling title of "present absentees." The UN refers to them as "internally displaced." So, we Palestinians are absent, present, internal, and displaced, all at the same time. Forgive us if we sometimes seem a bit confused.

Israel argues over the right of return of Palestinian refugees to Israel. But she also argues over the right of return of Palestinian refugees to a future Palestinian state in parts of the West Bank and Gaza. But why would Israel quarrel over the rights of refugees to return to a state she would have no sovereignty over? The answer is simple. It is because Israel has no intention of allowing any sort of Palestinian state to ever be established. As far as she is concerned, the whole of Palestine should be emptied of all Palestinians.

Finally, let us realize the most important aspect of the right of return. At its essence, the right of return is not one that can be negotiated away. It does not belong to the Palestinians collectively. Rather, it belongs individually to each of the almost 5 million registered Palestinian refugees walking the earth today.

And now I turn to Abbas. Last week, the Palestinian president told a group of 300 Israeli students visiting Ramallah, "We are not seeking to drown Israel with millions of refugees to change its structure." This was taken by many as a sign of Abbas' willingness to ease up on the right of return in negotiations with Israel. To those of us who have been keeping a close eye on Abbas, including his unwillingness to hold presidential elections for some time, his words came as no surprise. As a refugee himself, the Palestinian president is entitled to the same right as any of his brethren: to return to his

143

home or to be justly compensated. It seems that he has chosen the latter.

Israel doesn't just want our recognition, she NEEDS it!

March 29, 2014

The current negotiations between Israel and us Palestinians are essentially over. The whole episode was probably never going to yield anything real, but it was fun while it lasted.

We have witnessed the normal maneuvers by all the parties involved. The Americans said both sides needed to make compromises, while implicitly blaming the Palestinians for the failures. The Palestinians said that Israel's settlement building and continued discriminatory practices show that she is not serious about peace, all the while trying to cozy up more to the Americans, even getting a White House trip out of the deal. And Israel got to harp about terrorism and gutless Palestinian leadership, as her leaders peppered newscasts talking about annexation of the West Bank.

None of this was shocking to us. In fact, we Palestinians are surprised by almost nothing. Living with Israel already means living in a world where the bizarre is ordinary. It means existing in an alternate reality. Nothing stuns us. Many of those who have spoken to Palestinians might have observed this phenomenon. In fact, I am sure the following conversation took place many times over the past few weeks:

> *Non-Palestinian: Isn't it crazy how that Malaysian plane just disappeared?*
> *Palestinian: Not really.*
> *Non-Palestinian: How can you say that?*
> *Palestinian: Well, my homeland just "disappeared" too, so nothing sounds crazy to me.*

But this round of negotiations brought another curious (and quite odd) element into the Israeli-Palestinian dynamic. This time, Israel asked for something she has never asked for before. This time, she asked for something especially weird. This time, she asked, no, demanded, that in order for any talks to move forward, the Palestinians must recognize Israel as a "Jewish state."

145

Now, Israel has asked the Palestinian leadership for many things, and she has basically received them all, including denunciations of terrorism, the sidelining of opposition groups, and even general recognition. Palestinian leaders and negotiators like Mahmoud Abbas, Saeb Erekat, and Nabil Shaath have basically capitulated to the American/Israeli discourse of discussions that are supposedly leading to a two-state solution, which just about every Palestinian knows will never happen. But even these lackeys can't agree to this nonsense.

Also, we Palestinians have this pretty strong suspicion that Israel is not really interested in allowing us to have any sort of state at all, as evidenced by her continued land grabs, evictions, and confiscations, not to mention her incessant settlement activities.

So what is all this "recognize us the Jewish state" business really about? Is it a political ploy? Is Israel asking for something she knows the Palestinians will never give her just to put an end to this current round of talks? Some think that is the case. After all, what better way to kill the negotiations than to ask for something that is seemingly reasonable, only to have the Palestinians summarily reject it?

But what if that's not the case at all? Why would Israel need our recognition of her as a Jewish state? She already gets this acknowledgement from the United States of America, the most powerful country in the world, on a daily basis, unequivocally, from every politician, in every capacity. The declaration is a staple in the platforms of both the Republican and Democratic parties. They can't find a way to make our healthcare system better than Colombia's, or our education system better than New Zealand's, but they can easily figure out how to agree on this pronouncement, which, incidentally, has not made Americans any healthier or smarter. Even Great Britain has gotten in on the act lately, with David Cameron calling Israel "the nation-state of the Jewish people" during a trip there a couple of weeks ago.

With these two great powers on her side, what does Israel want with us? Why does she crave our recognition? Well, it's because she doesn't just *want* it. She *needs* it.

Israel can't move on without us. She needs us to tell her that everything is okay, that her actions these past 66 years have been acceptable, and that it was our fault, not hers. No, this recognition business is not some political ruse. Rather, it goes to the heart of the whole thing. Israel needs us to recognize her as the Jewish state so that she can feel better about

146

herself. The affirmation of every leader in the world won't mean anything unless we say it too.

Have you ever seen a wife argue passionately with her husband? She argues her points, and he argues his. Usually, the husband eventually relents and tells her, "I give up. You win. We'll have sushi for dinner." But sometimes that's not enough. She needs him to understand why she wants sushi, and why having sushi is just a better idea. She is not satisfied with winning the argument. She wants more. She needs more. She is not merely interested in his surrender. She needs his acquiescence, his agreement, and his consent. In other words, she needs his recognition.

Haven't you ever wondered if a failed relationship was actually your fault or not? Well, Israel is wondering the same thing. Basically, she needs us to tell her the one thing we all want to hear: "It not you, it's me."

If you think I am describing Israel as some sort of damaged, controlling psycho who needs everyone to agree with her, you'd be right.

There is a bright side here, though. If Israel needs our approval, we are not as insignificant as we have been telling ourselves we are. Israel actually cares what we think!

So, if it will move things along, I'll recognize Israel in whatever way she would like me to. I'll tell her, "It's not you, it's me." But just like everyone else who has ever uttered those words, I'm not going to mean it.

Jesus the Palestinian

April 20, 2014

I'm not a religious guy. I might talk about Jesus in a different way that priests, ministers, and popes do. I do not see him as the divine incarnate, and I'm not completely sure he saw himself that way either. But I do share one thing with my more religious friends. Jesus still lives for me today.

Jesus was one of us. We Palestinians are pretty proud of that. I've been to Bethlehem, Nazareth, and Jerusalem many times, and Palestinians, Muslim and Christian, are looking after Jesus' stuff pretty well.

And we see ourselves in his light.

Like us, he was told that he does not belong in Palestine. Like him, we remain.

Like us, he was told that his stories have no place there. Like him, we keep telling them, no matter the consequences.

Like us, he fought against unbridled power. Like him, we tell those who oppress us the hard truths they don't want to hear.

Like us, he gained supporters little by little. The most powerful shunned him at first. At the outset, only a few stood by him. But it won't take us 300 years to get an empire to agree with us, and it definitely shouldn't take us 2000 years to get 1.2 billion followers either. We have Facebook, Twitter, and everything else. Jesus never had those things. I mean, can you imagine Jesus' statuses?

- *Got kicked out of Jerusalem again today. Ugh.*
- *No justice, no peace!*
- *Hey guys, this pic is for everyone who said I couldn't walk on water.*
- *Could everyone please stop tagging me everywhere? The cops are looking for me!*
- *This was a rough week, I'm gonna be turning a lot of water into wine tonight, if you know what I mean.*

And let's get something straight here. Jesus did visit Lebanon, Jordan, and maybe even Egypt. But he never went to Rome or Greece, and he definitely never stepped foot in Britain. And I can say, unequivocally, unambiguously, and undeniably, that Jesus never visited America, no matter what anyone at Fox News might think. Jesus didn't have blond hair and blue eyes. Jesus was a Jew, but he wasn't from Poland, Russia, or New York City. He was from Nazareth, as I am, so he probably looked like me. Ok, he had flowing hair, and by all accounts, he was in really good shape, but you know what I mean.

So to everyone else out there in the world, we understand why you love Jesus too. You can borrow him, but you can't have him. He belongs to us.

I am not sure if Jesus arose from the dead after his execution. I am sure, however, that he had nothing to do with bunnies or eggs. And I'm also sure that we Palestinians today are preserving his message. The present-day natives of his land carry upon their shoulders Jesus' legacy of truth, rebellion, justice, suffering, abandonment, and, eventually, vindication. I am not certain if he was physically resurrected. But I am certain that he is alive today. Every Palestinian walking the earth today reminds me of that.

Jesus started it all. Like us, he walked the streets of Palestine, in constant persecution. And we say today the same words Jesus said 2000 years ago: Beware of our Truth.

I have always said that, as a Palestinian, I sleep well at night. And this Easter is no different. Yes, we struggle, we battle, we labor, we agonize, and we even die. But we have the truth. We have the guy who once said, "Remember that I am always with you, until the end of time." You see, Jesus is our secret weapon. And along with everything else that makes it awesome to be a Palestinian, that makes me feel pretty good.

149

The Pope saw Palestinians, and he likes us!

May 27, 2014

Pope Francis recently concluded his visit to the Holy Land. Now, I'm not a religious guy, but it doesn't matter, this pope likes me!

His visit was, of course, much more significant to us Palestinians than it was to Israelis. We like showing the reality of the situation to outsiders. Israel, well, she's not so crazy about it. We are Israel's dirty little secret, and, frankly, she would rather we just stay locked up and out of sight.

The pope went to Jerusalem and Bethlehem, and he even stopped for a moment at the separation wall. The New York Times reported, "Pope Francis touches the wall that divides Israel from the West Bank." Of course, the wall does not separate the West Bank from Israel. It separates the West Bank from the West Bank. Assuming he is literate, I would think Pope Francis is aware of this fact. As it turns out, the New York Times isn't.

But facts don't bother Israel and her supporters. Benjamin Netanyahu tried to pull a fast one on Francis. "Jesus was here, in this land. He spoke Hebrew," Netanyahu told Francis. The pope interrupted him. "Aramaic," he observed. "He spoke Aramaic, but he knew Hebrew," Netanyahu asserted. Now, Netanyahu is probably right. But saying Jesus spoke Hebrew is kind of like saying my dad speaks English. Sure, my dad knows English, but it's not how he expresses himself. If you really want to know what language someone speaks, you have to get him mad enough to curse. And I can tell you from experience, for my dad, it's not English.

And although I'm not in the business of dispensing advice to Benjamin Netanyahu, I feel compelled here. Bibi, I know you like arguing, but if you're going to quarrel with someone about the history of Jesus, you can literally pick no one worse than the pope. That's like arguing with Albert Einstein about gravity. You just don't do it.

Pope Francis, as is the custom in our part of the world, invited his hosts to his place some time in the future in return for their hospitality:

In this, the birthplace of the Prince of Peace, I wish to invite you, President Mahmoud Abbas, together with Israeli President Shimon Peres, to join me in heartfelt prayer to God for the gift of peace.

Some have interpreted this invitation to Peres as a snub to the leader of the Israeli government, Prime Minister Netanyahu. I hope they're right. If I were the pope, I wouldn't invite Netanyahu to my house either. Aside from being pretty imperialistic, racist, and violent, he just doesn't seem like a nice guy. Peres is no angel either, but if you have to pick between the two... well, it's a pretty easy decision. And while Abbas is not likely to add anything intelligent to any conversation, he will probably at least be respectful.

The Palestinian Authority has already said that Abbas will visit The Vatican. Israel has said that she appreciates the invitation but has made no commitment to actually make the visit. Let me be the first to make a bold prediction: Israel won't visit the pope. It would just be awkward. And I know how she feels. I have met many priests in my life, and I always worry about what they might think of me if they actually knew my resumé of sins. Well, Francis knows who Israel is. If I were in her shoes, I would stay home too.

Now, I followed Francis' visit closely. And maybe it was just me, but it seemed that whenever he was hanging out with Palestinians, he was happy and laughing. And whenever he was with Netanyahu, he was miserable and frowning. I think I even saw him check his watch. Bibi can have that effect on people. When he was with us, he looked like a guy at a party. When he was with Netanyahu, he looked like a guy at the dentist's office.

Now, it shouldn't be too surprising that the pope likes us. After all, Pope Francis and all his friends at The Vatican are spending their lives trying to live up to the standard of the most famous Palestinian of all time. And his visit allowed him to see how Jesus' cousins are living today.

He should visit more often.

Arabs "sheering" for the World Cup

June 18, 2014

An Arab should pick his or her favorite World Cup team carefully. But before I get into that, a quick word about Arabs and this year's festivities.

Soccer's premiere tournament makes almost every global citizen disconnect from the real world for a month every four years. Arabs are no exception. Additionally, this year, the last ten days or so of the World Cup will occur during the holy month of Ramadan, when Muslims fast from sunrise to sunset. Now, Ramadan is already a time of very low efficiency in the Arab world, and in this year's first week and a half of the holiday, as it intersects with the soccer frenzy, the region will be especially unproductive.

That means we should all not expect too much from the Arab world during that time. Gas prices should remain unchanged. Al-Qaeda will fall silent (even terrorists like soccer more than world domination). All hummus shipments to America will be delayed, unless you are buying Sabra, in which case I need to know where your store is located so I can begin my boycott campaign against you.

Ok, back to picking a World Cup team. By the way, many Arabs cannot pronounce "cheer" correctly. It comes out as "sheer." So, to my Arab comrades, if you are going to "sheer" for everyone this year, these are the rankings and guidelines I propose:

1. Algeria
Algerians are Arabs. They deserve our support more than anyone else for this reason alone. Also, when we curse at them for taking a bad shot, they will actually understand us.

2. Iran
Iranians are almost Arabs. They have the religion, the nose, and the skin tone. Also, white people think we are all the same anyway.

3. Spain
Of course, Spain is not an Arab country. But it used to be, for 700 years. It was, look it up.

4. Any African team
Remember when Qaddafi was the "King of Africa"? Ok, that was kind of a self-given title, but still, almost half of the Arab

152

League states are located in Africa, so sheering for Africans is highly encouraged.

5. Chile

Chile is home to the largest Palestinian community outside of the Arab world, estimated at 500,000 people. It is, look it up. Of course, Palestinians live all over the place, but that is another story for another day. There is even a soccer team in Chile called "Palestino," and its colors are red, green, and white. By my standards, that makes Chile pretty awesome. Sheer for Shile!

6. Portugal

Cristiano Rinaldo is so cute! But it's not because of his great body, slicked hair, or perfect teeth. No, it's because he has been vocal about Palestinian rights, even with the full knowledge that it might cost him. So if you're sheering for Portugal, that's perfectly fine.

7. Bosnia-Herzegovina

Bosnians aren't Arabs. And, as far as I know, almost no Arabs live there. But the country is over 50% Muslim, and, as a result, they show up to our Arab demonstrations. We can express our thanks by sheering for them.

8. Brazil

It is an Arab custom to respect your host, so Brazil is named here. Sheering for them is good manners.

9. Any Latino team

Through their relationship to Spain and the Spanish language, these guys are kind of like us too. They love the name Omar, and 20% of Spanish comes from Arabic. Did you know "Ole!" comes from "Yalla!"? It does!

10. Greece

Greeks are not Arabs, but most Greek restaurants do feature spinach pies and hummus. And they rival us for the hairiest men on the planet. Oh, and did you watch "My Big Fat Greek Wedding"? That could have easily been a movie about us.

11. Italy

Italians might be the only people in the world who move their hands when they talk more than we Arabs do. And like us, for them, yelling is an acceptable volume of normal conversation. So if you do sheer for them, make sure you do it loudly.

12. South Korea or Japan

You may sheer for these teams if you like, as they share our customs of drinking way too much tea and having a pile of outdoor shoes and indoor slippers at every exit of the house.

13. Russia

Russia seems to dislike just about everyone in the world, but they also seem to dislike us a little bit less than they dislike everyone else. So, sheer for them at your own risk.

14. Any white country not named America, France, or England

White soccer teams just seem out of place, don't they? Also, they don't kiss each other on the cheek when they score, so I just don't understand them.

15. America

Well, this is a complicated one. As an American, I want to sheer for my country. But when I remember that bombing Arabs is on the platform of basically every politician here, I realize that I can't. Although we Arab Americans have contributed to America for over a hundred years and done very well here, we find ourselves constantly having to prove that we love this country. We love America, but she needs to love us back. Oh, and the $3 billion a year to Israel make my sheering for them Arab-ly impossible.

16. France or England

Well, if you are an Arab and you are supporting France or England, please decolonize yourself quickly. Their carving up of our lands a hundred years ago created sectarianism and conflict that we are still dealing with today. Our problems are our own, but France and England stirred the pot. If you are sheering for them, go read a book.

Now, there are some teams I would have included high on my list if they had made the World Cup. For example, I would have loved to sheer for India, but c'mon, one billion people and you can't find 23 good soccer players?

So, there it is. Sheer however you like, but if you follow these rules, your Arabness will stay fully intact.

Thank God Tariq is one of us

July 9, 2014

Over the past week, the American press has latched on to the story of Tariq Khdeir, the 15-year-old Palestinian American whose beating at the hands of Israeli police in Jerusalem was caught on video for the world to see.

CNN couldn't get enough. Wolf Blitzer interviewed Tariq's aunt on national television. Much to the surprise of viewers, she spoke perfect English, accent-free.

And CNN wasn't alone in its fascination:

The New York Times: Beating of Palestinian-American Boy Caught on Video
Huffington Post: Tariq Abu Khdeir Was Beaten By Israeli Police
USA Today: Family of teen beaten in Israel pleads for his return
Los Angeles Times: American teen beaten in Mideast is a cousin of slain Palestinian

The US State Department even got in on the reporting, saying that it could "confirm that Tariq Khdeir, an American citizen, is being held by Israeli authorities in Jerusalem." It even noted that it was "profoundly troubled" by reports that Tariq was "severely beaten," calling for "a speedy, transparent and credible investigation and full accountability for any excessive use of force." (Read the full State Department statement here)

Tariq is getting a lot of attention. And his government is asking for accountability. Of course, it's not because he is a Palestinian. No, it's because he is an American. It's because he lives in Florida. It's because while he is one of "them," he is also one of "us." And thank God for that.

See, if Tariq wasn't one of us, he would be just like one of the over 1,500 Palestinian children killed by Israeli forces since 2000. If he were not a high school sophomore in Tampa, he would be just like one of the 37 children killed in Israel's 2012 bombing campaign of Gaza, Operation Pillar of Defense. If he were not a normal American kid who listened to hip hop music, he would have been just like one of the 352 children killed in Israel's December 2008 offensive, Operation Cast Lead. If he were not one of us, he might be just like the 8 children killed so far in Israel's current Gaza attack, Operation Protective Edge. See, when Israel names an operation, she means business.

If Tariq were not an American, he would be just like Mustafa Tamimi. Mustafa was killed in 2011 after being shot in the head at close range by a tear gas canister. He lived in Nabi Saleh, a West Bank village that has been protesting weekly against Israeli confiscation of its land. An investigation was commenced, and while Israel found Mustafa's death to be "regrettable," she found no fault, except for that of Mustafa, of course. "Tamimi put himself at unnecessary risk, unfortunately resulting in his death." She also found that "the shooting of the canister was done in accordance with the relevant rules and regulations." See, in Israel, there are rules about how you shoot a tear gas canister at a Palestinian guy less than ten meters away from you.

If Tariq were not an American, he would be just like Iman El-Hams. 13-year-old Iman was killed in 2004 when she was shot 17 times near a checkpoint in Gaza. Iman was walking near a checkpoint carrying a bag when Israeli soldiers spotted her. After shooting her bag to confirm that it did not contain explosives, Iman began to run away. Although the soldiers on the scene had confirmed that she was a child, she was shot as she tried to run away. After falling to the ground, she approached by an Israeli soldier who shot her more than a dozen more times to "confirm the kill." After numerous investigations, the soldier was found guilty of nothing, even though he said he would have done the same had it been a 3-year-old child. Oh, and Iman's bag contained a bunch of textbooks. The soldier was promoted in rank and compensated for his defense expenditures. Israel found that he had not fallen afoul of the law. See, in Israel there are rules about how you repeatedly shoot a Palestinian girl carrying a bookbag near a checkpoint.

If Tariq weren't like us, we might have never heard his name. But Tariq is an American, so he will get our attention. And getting attention means getting justice, right? Well, not necessarily. While Israeli officials have made it clear that they will investigate the "allegations" of police brutality (there's clear video evidence by the way, so you really have to have a lot of chutzpah to call it "allegations"), they have also made it clear that they will continue to investigate Tariq, who they say might have been throwing rocks. It sounds ridicu-

156

lous, unless you remember that in Israel, rock thrower vs. tank = fair fight.

And let us not forget the case of another American who once showed solidarity with us Palestinians. Rachel Corrie was crushed to death by an American-made, Israeli-driven bulldozer in Gaza in 2003, as she protested the indiscriminate destruction of Palestinian homes. Her death was investigated, and no one was found responsible, despite numerous eyewitness accounts that the operator of the machine must have seen her before running her over. Israel said that Rachel and her partners in the International Solidarity Movement were acting "irresponsibly." See, Israel even has rules for how you drive your bulldozer over a woman directly in front of you.

Even more alarming than the Israeli refusal to dispense justice (which was predictable) was the official American disinclination to push Israel for a real investigation (which was sadly predictable as well). If America was not willing to push Israel after the depraved killing of a white Christian woman from Washington, what would ever make me think my government would even nudge her after the simple beating of a brown Muslim kid from Florida?

Tariq's passport might mean more cameras in his face, but it won't mean more justice. But for now, I'll take the cameras. It's more than I'm used to.

Israel never surprises me

July 16, 2014

No one else can understand a Palestinian's relationship to Israel, and I wouldn't expect as much. She consumes us, in every sense you can imagine.

As a result, we have an astounding sense of familiarity with her. See, sometimes a victim knows his tormenter better than the tormentor knows herself. Nothing she does surprises us.

I am not surprised to see Israelis sitting on hills in a city near Gaza, watching the Israeli missiles fall. One onlooker called it "just good fun." Others were eating popcorn, which is not surprising. If you're sick enough to be entertained by watching hi-tech missiles fall on an open-air prison in one of the most densely populated places on the planet, it doesn't really shock me if you bring along some snacks to pass the time.

I am not surprised that the news reporter on the scene also noted that some of the "audience" were smoking hookahs. I do take some offense to that. Hookahs belong to us. But I'm not surprised. If you're sick enough to pretend that you didn't steal another people's land, it doesn't really shock me that you can smoke their bongs without a second thought.

I am not surprised when Benjamin Netanyahu calls for revenge on his Twitter feed after the discovery of the bodies of the three Israeli Jewish teens in late June. Predictably, less than two days later, Palestinian teen Muhammad Abu Khdeir was abducted in East Jerusalem as he waited in the early morning hours for prayer outside a mosque in the opening days of Ramadan. Not unexpectedly, his body was found the next day in a Jerusalem forest. An autopsy revealed that he was burned alive. His murderers have been arrested and are pleading insanity. They will, we expect, spend a nominal amount of time incarcerated before they are deemed sane enough to return to Israeli society. It's not going to shock me when they spend less time in jail than a Palestinian who hurls a stone at an Israeli tank.

I am not surprised when Ayelet Shaked advocates calling Palestinians "little snakes." Oh, she also advocated the destruction of "elderly and its women, its cities and its villages, its property and its infrastructure." Oh, she is also a member of the Israeli Knesset. Oh, she is also a member of the ruling coalition of Netanyahu's government. Oh, and the prime minister had nothing to say about her call to genocide. Oh, and her Facebook post calling for all of these things got over 5,100 likes. If a society is sick enough to elect and promote a fascist into the highest levels of political office, it doesn't really shock me when her murderous rants are met with nothing.

We Palestinians, unfortunately, are not taken aback by anything that Israel does.

The only thing that has changed in Israel in recent years is that the right-wingers are much more comfortable spewing their hatred than ever before. This upsets those on the Israeli left. The leftists are much more accustomed to packaging their revulsion of the Palestinians in a much more acceptable manner. But it seems they are letting those on the right have their way for now. Maybe it will work, they think. After all, they all want the same thing. This has been known to us for some time. It's not too extraordinary to us.

I am not surprised when CNN, America's moderate and balanced news network, continues to depict the conflict as one between two equal entities. If viewers didn't know any better, they might think there is a country called Israel and a country called Palestine and they are fighting each other. That kind of misinformation and skewed coverage is routine for us.

Finally, I am not surprised when Israel tells the world she is "notifying" residents in Gaza before dropping a bomb on their house. She says that is "humane." I've heard it all before. But if you're going after Hamas commanders, why even warn them at all? Their wives and kids are fair game anyway. It's our fault for living in that place to begin with.

So, we will still be around when this is all over. And Israel will have bought herself some more time to continue maintaining the status quo. It's fine. We're fine. We'll get through it.

Being a form of entertaining target practice for a society that wants us exterminated anyway is nothing new. We're used to it. Don't feel bad for us. It's normal.

Palestinians need to act appropriately

July 19, 2014

Over the past couple of weeks, many of us Palestinians have been incessantly writing, posting, tweeting, and commenting about Palestine, Israel, and Gaza. I have been no exception. On July 9, I posted "Thank God Tariq is one of us," my take on how the American media and public can only connect with the beating of a Palestinian when he is an American. And on July 15, I wrote "Israel never surprises me," a cynical description of how we Palestinians have become all too accustomed to Israel's treatment of us as subhuman.

As a result of those two writings, I received many messages from Jews, both Israeli and American. Most of them were hate-filled and racist. I am used to those. They don't bother me at all. But I received many more with a different feel.

Many Jewish friends, acquaintances, and former students wrote me with a similar theme:

"Amer, why are you being so polarizing?"
"Shouldn't we all just want peace?"
"Why don't you seek harmony?"

Should I avoid being polarizing? Not if it makes people think. Should I advocate for peace? That's kind of a silly thing to ask. Do I seek harmony? I had to think about that one. And I have finally come up with a response: "Not yet."

Now that I have answered those questions to the best of my ability, let me get to why I think these kinds of things are being asked of me at all. First, many Jews, many more than ever before, are reassessing their personal relationship with Israel. That is a good thing. And it has nothing to do with any activity on the part of Palestinians, unless you classify survival as an activity. Those who are seeking peace, reconciliation, and understanding might be naive at this point. But at least, it seems, we have moved past "A land without a people for a people without a land." But secondly, and more importantly, many Jews believe that Palestinians should be acting in a certain way. Some ask for acquiescence, capitulation, and surrender. Some want us to apologize. And some want us to simply disappear. Of course, Palestinians cannot provide any of those things.

But those who consider themselves liberal Zionists or mainstream Jewish supporters of Israel ask for something that they believe Palestinians can and should give them: accommodation. They want peace of mind. They want me to tell them that everything is OK.

Well, it's not.

After the murderous burning-alive of Muhammad Abu Khdeir in Jerusalem as he was waiting for morning prayers, forgive me I couldn't find it in my heart to say, "Give peace a chance." After the Gaza beach massacre of the four Bakr boys, Zakaria, Ahed, Mohammed, and Ismail, as they were playing soccer, forgive me if I couldn't bring myself to say, "Can't we all just get along?" And after the brutal slaughter of three more Palestinian boys, the Shahebars, Jihad, Fullah, and Wasim, who were feeding pigeons on their roof, forgive me if I didn't feel kinship, cooperation, and understanding.

Maybe they thought Muhammad had an ominous reason to be in front of that mosque. Or maybe they thought the Bakr boys were launching rockets from their feet. Or maybe, just maybe, they thought the Shahebars were training the pigeons to attack Tel Aviv. There, am I now being "understanding" enough for you?

One might imagine, in light of all this, that a Palestinian might not feel harmonious at all. I can think of many other emotions that might be more appropriate:

Rage.
Anger.
Defiance.
Sarcasm.
Contempt.
Fear.
Spite.
Anxiety.
Concern.
Dread.
Violation.
Loss.
Abandonment.
Despair.
Panic.
Terror.

But not "harmony"... definitely not "harmony."

Israel, listen, I know what I'm talking about

July 20, 2014

Israel,

Don't you see what is going on? I won. It's over.

There are protests around the world, all in support of me. None for you. It's clear. Last week, within 5 days of each other, I attended two demonstrations in Detroit, each garnering over 1000 people. Today, over 5,000 walked through the streets of Chicago calling you out. Remember when you had Chicago in your pocket? Not anymore. 15,000 in London marched against you. And it wasn't just us. There were white people, black people... even Jews! You believe that? New York, San Francisco, Berlin, Madrid... everywhere. They came out in the tens of thousands in Johannesburg, Durban, and Cape Town. That's right, South Africa. And those guys know what they're talking about.

Over a million people around the world, and we didn't have to bribe them or anything. We didn't lobby them. We didn't threaten them. They just joined with us, all on their own. I guess you might just say that they are all wrong and misguided. But no one is buying it anymore. Those days are over.

It must be scary. It's been a good run of 66 years. But it's finished. Things will never be like they used to be.

But don't worry, I am here for you. Believe it or not, I am the key to your redemption. It's not too late. You have to open yourself to learning from me, because, as has become all too clear, I am just better at getting the world to like me than you are.

You know how I did it? I didn't act like a jerk. Sure, I made mistakes, a lot of them. But I just wasn't a jerk. Actually, as it turns out, as long as you're not a jerk, people will be pretty open to you.

But you've been kind of a jerk for a long time. Someone has to give it to you straight. And no one knows you better than I do. Let's talk about some of your jerk-like activities.

Shooting a teenager with an M-16 when he throws a rock at you. Jerky.

Bulldozing villages to make way for your immigrants that you could have easily housed somewhere else. Really jerky.

Hiding behind your big, rich, influential friend whenever you do something wrong. Jerky, and kinda sad.

Claiming hummus and falafel as staples of Israeli cuisine. C'mon. It doesn't get jerkier than that.

Dropping leaflets in a neighborhood full of civilians telling them you are going to attack in two days, and then still massacring them when they don't leave... well, aside from being just plain mean and murder-y, that's something that only a major jerk would do.

Don't you know threats are much more effective when you use them to get what you want instead of actually following through? Iran has perfected this. So has the United States. And no one does it better than Arab moms.

By the way, I have a couple more things to say about the whole dropping-leaflets-in-Gaza-to-warn-them thing. First, how are they supposed to learn from your threats if you just kill them all? You never thought of that, did you? Also, the whole "previous warning" thing doesn't make you less of a jerk. FYI.

In any case, you should probably run most of your stuff by me before you actually go through with it. I have a pretty good sense of how the world thinks about you and these things. I'm not trying to be cocky or anything. Sure, you can kill better than I can. But in everything else, I'm just better. Most of all, I'm just not a jerk.

Yours truly,
Amer, your Palestinian friend

To Jon Stewart... thanks, and no thanks

July 23, 2014

Dear Jon,

I, like many Americans, watch you just about every day. You're welcome. I'm not sure if you know this, and I'm not sure if you intended it, but you have become somewhat of a hero among us Palestinians. Your analyses about Palestine/Israel are fair, levelheaded, and funny. In fact, those are the exact words I used when I wrote you a letter back in November 2009. Actually, your interview way back then with Mustafa Barghouti and Anna Baltzer was the subject of the very first post on "The Civil Arab." Yes, something you aired on The Daily Show inspired the birth of an Arab American blog. Thanks.

A few days ago, my fellow Palestinian American comedian and political analyst Dean Obeidallah penned an article for the Daily Beast titled, "How Jon Stewart Made It Okay to Care About Palestinian Suffering." In that piece, Dean detailed how you helped to humanize Palestinians, making it okay to not only care about us, but also to say it out loud. He summed up your effect:

The seeds Stewart has planted over the years have taken root and are starting to blossom. And here's why that's a good thing for all. Stewart's message is truly one of empathy—something often missing in discussions of this conflict. Too often, people view this contest as a zero sum game where even the slightest acknowledgment that the other side is suffering is an attack upon their own side.

You are an influential American voice. And you are a Jew, so your words about our part of the world carry a certain sort of gravity that would never accompany Bill O'Reilly or his ilk. Also, you seem to understand that the Palestinian-Israeli conflict is chiefly characterized by a power dynamic. And we all know you are not shy to challenge those in power to be more honest and fair.

So, in the name of all Palestinians living around the world (and trust me, we really do live around the world), thank you.

164

Without you, we would undoubtedly be portrayed in the media much more terribly than we already are. As a sign of my thanks, I'd like to send you a copy of my book, "Being Palestinian Makes Me Smile." Incidentally, I am available to come on your show and talk about it whenever you like.

But there's something else. I'm a little worried. Progressive liberals see you as their beacon, someone who speaks the truth in a media world where deception and misdirection are the norm. And speaking the truth, funny enough, is a tough enterprise. But is also something that cannot be done incompletely, piece by piece.

The Palestinian struggle is not simply characterized by the West Bank and Gaza. It is not simply characterized by the deaths in Gaza over the past few weeks. It is not simply about being seen as human beings who are worthy of the most basic of rights. No, it is about justice, about equity. We Palestinians do not just seek to stop being killed and dispossessed. We ask for much more than that.

The roots of our grievances are quite elementary. Basically, white Europeans came to Palestine, stole our lands, and kicked us out. That's why I'm in America. The people that did that to us could have been anybody. They just happened to be Jews. Then, they proceeded to create a society and set of laws characterized by ethnic supremacy, attempting to ensure that Palestinians never again have a claim to their ancestral homeland. But we Palestinians are pesky. We don't go away all that easily. So we are still a thorn in their sides 66 years later.

That's it, simple as that. It's a colonial enterprise. I mean, the government spokesperson has an Australian accent. You can hear it when he is speaking on behalf of the American-accented prime minister.

We ask for the right of return, the addressing of our grievances, and the telling of our story. Sounds pretty just, right? Can you stand with us on those things too? Can you say openly that Palestinians have as at least as much of a claim to all of Palestine/Israel as Jews do? Can you say that we deserve to be treated as equal citizens regardless of religion or ethnicity?

See, we Palestinians all carry around a map of our homeland, whether it's embodied on a necklace, on a tattoo, or in our hearts. And yes, it's from the "river to the sea." And yes, we know that those borders were drawn by imperial powers from Europe. But it is that recognizable triangular New Jersey-sized piece of land from which we form our political iden-

165

tity. That's where we were driven from. That's where we fight for justice. That's where we find our roots. That map is why we call ourselves Palestinian.

And guess what? Israelis draw the same map. In fact, the Israeli Ministry of Tourism publishes a map that does not delineate the border between Israel and the West Bank at all. Funny, right? That could be a segment on The Daily Show. The fact that Palestinians and Israelis draw each other's countries into their own maps is easy fodder.

Perhaps you're taking a step-by-step approach where you will eventually get to the larger issues around this "conflict." If so, I would advise you to do so secretly. If word gets out about that, you might not last too long on the air.

My point to you is this. In a country where we are seen as generally unworthy of protection, we appreciate you telling the world that we Palestinians are, in fact, human beings who do not deserve to be indiscriminately killed. But it is not enough. My worry is that your saying (or implying) as much will lead other liberal, progressive Americans of conscience to think it is enough as well.

Now, I'm not necessarily asking you to raise the "Zionism is racism" banner. However, if you want to, I have many in my possession and will happily send you one. Let me know. I'm just asking you to say that the current carnage in Gaza might be indicative of a larger problem where the "only democracy in the Middle East" sees us natives as a "demographic threat."

So, can you say any of these things? If so, thanks. If you can't bring yourself to do it, I am always available to come on and have a discussion. I'll bring a map.

Sincerely,
Amer

What is Netanyahu up to?

July 30, 2014

If you've been observing, following, and analyzing Israel, especially in its current offensive in Gaza, you might be asking a central question: What exactly is Israeli Prime Minister Benjamin Netanyahu doing?

Aren't his orders that have resulted in the destruction of entire neighborhoods unnecessary? Aren't his directives that have led to the annihilation of media outlets, humanitarian outposts, and Gaza's main power plant severe and irrational? Aren't his commands that have caused the deaths of over 1600 Palestinians, 80% of them civilians, extreme, disproportionate, and excessive?

If he really wanted to stop the rocket fire, couldn't he just continue to pluck them from the sky with his Iron Dome, as he is so effectively doing right now, finding a political way to sideline Hamas without firing a shot? If he really wanted to destroy the tunnels that snaked into Israeli territory, couldn't he destroy or cap them from the Israeli side to prevent anyone from coming through?

If he were really interested in the decay of Hamas, why wouldn't he allow the Palestinian unity government to form, a process that would most likely lead to a quieter and more marginalized Hamas? If he wanted to stop terrorism, why would he continue to bombard the innocents of Gaza, a move that every analyst in the world knows will only fuel Hamas' popularity?

You would not be too crazy to ask these questions. In fact, posing these sorts of inquiries might seem entirely normal... entirely normal, that is, if you weren't a Palestinian.

To us Palestinians, what Benjamin Netanyahu is doing comes as no surprise. To me, as a child of Palestinian refugees driven from their ancestral homes by Israel, the Israeli prime minister is simply doing what all his predecessors have. The story of Palestinians is personified by despair after despair, anguish after anguish, refuge after refuge.

Since its establishment in 1948, Israel's posture has been to see us Palestinians as outsiders, as foreign, as a threat. I do not expect anyone else to understand what it is like to be viewed as a menace in your own homeland, to be denied sim-

167

ple humanity on the lands of your grandfathers, to be labeled as a "demographic threat" by a group of outsiders who hate your existence but seemingly love your food.

But we live this. And we cannot escape it. Being Palestinian is relentless. It is about relentlessly enduring, attempting to outlive our oppression.

This isn't about Gaza. This isn't about Hamas. This isn't about a missing soldier. This isn't about thousands of slaughtered Palestinians. This isn't about tunnels. This isn't about rockets. This isn't about demilitarizing Gaza.

It is about something much bigger, yet quite simple. To us, it is about survival.

That strong sense of identity informs how we see the current war. We Palestinians do not see Gaza as a specific conflict in its time and place, but rather as another phase in Israel's ongoing attempts to ethnically cleanse us and drive us from our lands.

The current massive non-violent marches and rallies in the West Bank and Israel by Palestinians are not simply being undertaken to protest the Israeli atrocities in Gaza. To think as much would be to misunderstand Palestinian identity entirely. They are about resistance to occupation, racism, and dispossession. They are part of the Palestinian narrative, which is precisely why they have been so violently repressed. Tens of thousands have marched peacefully in the face of live ammunition, fired by a military that cares not if it kills them. Human beings do not demonstrate and die in search of hate. They do it in search of freedom.

They do it to protest an Israeli tradition that has told them things like:

A Jewish state on only part of the land is not the end, but on the beginning... A Jewish state must be established immediately, even if it is only in part of the country. The rest will follow in the course of time. David Ben-Gurion (1937)

and...

There is no such thing as a Palestinian people... It is not as if we came and threw them out and took their country. Golda Meir (1969)

and...

[The Palestinians] are beasts walking on two legs. Menachem Begin (1982)

and...

The past leaders of our movement left us a clear message to keep Eretz Israel from the Sea to the River Jordan for future generations. Yitzhak Shamir (1990)

and...

Israel should have exploited the repression of the demonstrations in China, when world attention focused on that country, to carry out mass expulsions among the Arabs of the territories. Benjamin Netanyahu (1989)

and...

It is the duty of Israeli leaders to explain to public opinion, clearly and courageously, a certain number of facts that are forgotten with time. The first of these is that there is no Zionism, colonialization, or Jewish State without the eviction of the Arabs and the expropriation of their lands. Ariel Sharon (1998)

and...

Israel may have the right to put others on trial, but certainly no one has the right to put the Jewish people and the State of Israel on trial. Ariel Sharon (2001)

and this, by Zionism's founding father:

Spirit the penniless population across the frontier by denying it employment... Both the process of expropriation and the removal of the poor must be carried out discreetly and circumspectly. Theodor Herzl (1895)

The Israeli assault on Gaza, the crackdown on Palestinians marching nonviolently, and all the previous onslaughts on our narrative are nothing more than a punishment for not accepting complete Israeli hegemony. It is precisely because we have not capitulated that we are being slain. It is because we have not forgotten. It is because we have survived.

What is most important to understand is that Benjamin Netanyahu is trying to achieve specifically what Zionism requires of him: the abolition of Palestinian civilization.

169

The accents of the Israeli team

August 5, 2014

For many, following all the ins and outs of the Israeli-Palestinian saga can be confusing. Hamas did that, the Israeli army did that. They started the war. No, they started the war. They broke the ceasefire. No, they broke the ceasefire. Hummus belongs to them. No, it belongs to them.

It is all very overwhelming. One thing, however, is glaringly clear. American journalists seem to have a much easier time having conversations with Israeli officials than they do with their Palestinian counterparts. The reason is obvious. All of Israel's official mouthpieces speak perfect unaccented English. And why wouldn't they? After all, they are not from Israel.

Peter Lerner is the foreign press spokesperson for the Israel Defense Forces. He was born in London in 1973. He immigrated to Israel in 1985. Hebrew, one of the two official languages of Israel (yes, Arabic is an official language too, because Israel is a democracy), is his second language. You might have wondered why Peter Lerner sounds more like a spokesperson for the Queen than he does for Israel. Why wouldn't he? He is, after all, a foreigner in the land of Israel.

Dore Gold is a diplomat who has served in many Israeli governments. He was once Israel's ambassador to the United Nations. He is currently the president of an Israeli think tank in Jerusalem. He was born in Connecticut, attended high school in Massachusetts, and earned a BA, MA, and PhD from Columbia University in New York City. He has appeared on television numerous times during Israel's latest offensive defending and explaining the policies of the Netanyahu government. As you might expect, his English is perfect. Mr. Gold lives in Jerusalem. He might even live in a house that once belonged to Palestinians. Of course, I don't know that for sure, but trust me, in Jerusalem, it's a safe bet. You might have wondered why Dore Gold sounds like a Yankees fan. Why wouldn't he? He is, after all, a foreigner in the land of Israel.

Mark Regev is the official spokesman of the Netanyahu government. In 1960, he was born in Australia, where he grew up and finished college. He immigrated to Israel at the

170

age of 22, when he began his graduate studies at the Hebrew University of Jerusalem. He has remained in his adopted homeland ever since. Hebrew is also his second language. You might have wondered why the official Israeli spokesman sounds like Crocodile Dundee. Why wouldn't he? He is, after all, a foreigner in the land of Israel.

Michael Oren was most recently Israel's ambassador to the United States. He was born in upstate New York. He earned his MA and PhD from Princeton University in New Jersey. He immigrated to Israel in his mid-twenties. He has lectured at dozens of American campuses. He articulately defends Israeli policies on American televisions across our great country. Well, he is usually articulate, if you don't count his recent interview on MSNBC when he suddenly (and quite conveniently) couldn't hear Andrea Mitchell when she asked him about reports that Israel had eavesdropped on John Kerry last year. But even when he flusters and fumbles, he speaks eloquent East Coast English. You might have wondered why Michael Oren sounds like an American university professor. Why wouldn't he? He is, after all, a foreigner in the land of Israel.

Micky Rosenfeld is the Israeli police spokesperson to the foreign press. He speaks English flawlessly. That's because he is English. Yup, he was born in England and grew up there. He is blond and blue-eyed. There's nothing wrong with that, of course. He grew up with Duran Duran, the English Premiere League, and bland food. The garlicky cuisine of his new homeland must have come as a bit of a shock to him. You might have wondered why Micky Rosenfeld sounds like Piers Morgan. Why wouldn't he? He is, after all, a foreigner in the land of Israel.

Ron Dermer is Israel's current ambassador to the United States of America. He has been all over CNN in recent weeks. He attended the University of Pennsylvania before moving to Israel is his twenties. He was born in 1971 in Miami Beach, where both his father and brother were once the mayor there. He is one of Netanyahu's closest advisers, writing many of his speeches, in English I assume. He is highly educated, yet for some reason he still sounds obnoxious and rude during just about every interview. You might have wondered why Ron Dermer sounds like a whiny kid from Florida. Why wouldn't he? He is, after all, a foreigner in the land of Israel.

Now I don't really mind that all of these Israeli messengers speak perfect English in American, Australian, and British accents. However, I do mind that with all that Western education they still can't pronounce "Hamas." They insist on continuing to say "Khamas." This is just offensive. Hamas is already frightening enough with its crappy rockets, ancient rifles, and hooded militants. Do they really have to add that chilling "kha" sound? Do they do that with all "h" sounds? It would make some nursery rhymes seem just downright scary. "Khumpty Dumpty sat on a wall" just sounds alarming. C'mon guys. It's "Hamas," like "happy." Just think that. Hamas. Happy. Hamas. Happy. See, it works.

In any case, this is the cast of characters acting as Israel's cheerleaders to the American public. Justifying racial supremacy, ethnic cleansing, and indiscriminate bombing campaigns definitely sounds better when it's done in an accent we can all relate to. But I'm sure every American listening to them still wonders why all these Israelis sound like the next door neighbor. Why wouldn't they? They are, after all, foreigners in the land of Israel. Foreign colonist settlers.

Being black, being Palestinian

August 17, 2014

It is hard for me to see Ferguson through anything other than Palestinian eyes.

The killing of 18-year-old Michael Brown, as he was unarmed and reportedly surrendering, has triggered protests in Missouri against aggressive police action. The protests have been met, quite expectedly, with aggressive police action. This aggressive police action will be met with more protests, and on and on we go. Sound familiar?

The similiarities between Ferguson and Palestine are stark. Shared experiences, sentiments, and anger abound. As it turns out, being black here and being Palestinian over there aren't really that different.

As black Americans filled the streets of Ferguson to decry what they saw as the unjustified killing of one of their young men, they were met by an over-militarized police presence looking to crush them. Sound familiar?

Their protests were welcomed with tear gas and rubber bullets. Sound familiar?

Well, it sounds familiar to us, so familiar that many Palestinians took to Twitter to advise their American counterparts in Ferguson on how to deal with such attacks. We saw tweets like, "Remember to not touch your face when tear-gassed or put water on it." And, "Always make sure to run against the wind /to keep calm when you're teargassed, the pain will pass, don't rub your eyes!" And my personal favorite, "Don't keep much distance from the police, if you're close to them they can't tear gas." Yes, we Palestinians are very creative when it comes to anti-anti-protesting. We are professional protestors.

Something interesting happened on CNN on Friday. As Don Lemon was reporting from a crowd of Ferguson's black citizens (who make up 67% of the city's population), he went from individual to individual, taking opinions and testimony. As the mic was being passed around, the overwhelming sentiments expressed were those of suspicion, mistrust, and skepticism of the police. Citizen after citizen expressed anger at how the police pointed to Brown's alleged criminal activity, dehumanizing him in a way that seemed like it was tailored to somehow justify the actions of a police officer who shot an

173

unarmed citizen who was reportedly surrendering, with his hands up. It got even more bizarre when, a few hours later, the police then announced that Darren Wilson, the police officer who shot Brown, had no idea that the young black man he had stopped had any possible connection to a crime. Blaming the victim, justifying excessive force, and outright lying are things a Palestinian sees from the Israeli government on a daily basis.

But what seemed most familiar to me was how the black residents there lacked a particular emotion regarding a white police officer killing a young black citizen, leaving his body laying in the street for hours. They weren't shocked, not even a little bit. They clearly felt sad, angry, and disenfranchised. But they weren't shocked or surprised. I know how that feels. Or how it doesn't feel.

Above all, the most obvious and discernible resemblance between Palestine and Ferguson is the one that is the most chilling of all. On the night after Brown's death, black protesters filled the streets of Ferguson. A local officer was caught on tape, bellowing at the citizens flowing onto the streets, "Bring it... all you f---ing animals, bring it." Similarly, Israeli soldiers have been known to pass time by placing Palestinian children in their crosshairs and boast about how many more they have killed. In Ferguson, there is at least one too many officers who sees black protestors as animals, and in Israel, there are least two too many soldiers who see Palestinians in the same way.

As one Palestinian put it on Twitter, "The Palestinian people know what it means to be shot while unarmed because of your ethnicity."

It's bad enough when someone sees you as a creature unworthy of the most basic of human protections. It's infinitely worse when that someone is also pointing a gun at you. There is nothing scarier than that. If you're wondering what that might feel like, ask a black American... or a Palestinian. Either way, you'll get the same answer.

The occupier has no clothes!

September 4, 2014

We all remember Hans Christian Andersen's short tale, "The Emperor's New Clothes," the story about two weavers who promise an emperor a new suit of clothes that is invisible on those who are "hopelessly stupid." At the end of the story, the vain emperor parades before his subjects in his new (invisible) clothes. As the fearful, cheerful crowd keeps up the charade, a child, too innocent to lie, loudly announces, "But he isn't wearing anything at all!" The rest of the crowd, inspired by the child's courage, begin to take on his cry as well. The emperor, quivering at the notion that he is exposed, continues his procession nonetheless.

This past Sunday on CNN, Brian Stelter, the host of "Reliable Sources," interviewed Israeli analyst and former journalist Matti Friedman. The topic was Friedman's latest article on Tablet, "An Insider's Guide to the Most Important Story on Earth," where the writer, a former Jerusalem-based reporter for the Associated Press, attempted to explain how and why reporters are fixated on the happenings in Israel, the West Bank, and Gaza. He laid out the reasons as to why, as CNN's tagline put it, there exists a "disproportionate focus" on Israel.

Friedman starts out by telling us that this summer's events in Gaza were not especially important or unique, as these things have happened before and will happen again. I will eventually get to whether or not that characterization is accurate. But it is important to note how he, a former journalist who uses that experience precisely to give himself legitimacy in this article, describes the Gaza war of the summer of 2014:

> *People were killed, most of them Palestinians, including many unarmed innocents.*

This is what I would call "truthful deception." Supporters of Israeli policies are usually quite adept at this particular skill. "Truthful deception" is saying or writing something technically accurate, even perhaps sounding like a concession, that is still actually misleading or incomplete. One might expect a husband to engage in this sort of treachery, but one

175

would hope for much more from a journalist, even a former one.

Again:

People were killed, most of them Palestinians, including many unarmed innocents.

People are supposed to read this and say, "Wow, a supporter of Israel is saying that?! He must be honest!"

According to the United Nations, 96.5% of the deaths in this summer's Gaza War (including Israeli soldiers) were those of Palestinians (2,104 out of 2,179). "Most" means "majority." "Majority" means "more than half the total." 96.5% is not "most." 96.5% is "almost all." Sure, in this statement, "most" might be technically accurate, but it's not precise, sincere, or complete. When you hear "most," you don't think, "Oh, he must mean 96.5%."

Also, 70% of the Palestinian deaths were those of unarmed innocents, including 495 children. "Many" means "numerous." "Many" doesn't necessarily suggest any sort of relative proportion to the total. 70% is not "many." Actually, 70% is "most." Sure, "many" might be technically accurate, but, again, it's not precise, sincere, or complete. When you hear "many," you don't think, "Oh, he must mean 70%."

Friedman does not use any statistics in his assessment. And why would he? It would have sounded quite different if he had written, "People were killed, almost all of them Palestinians, most of them unarmed innocents." But Friedman, who is attempting to make a point about journalistic integrity, is not interested in being specific here. He is practicing "truthful deception."

He does it again later in the article when he speaks of the media's mischaracterization of Israel's settlement policy. Before deriding the media for portraying settlements as a cause of the conflict rather than a symptom (a distinction without a difference in this case), he says he believes the policy is "a serious moral and strategic error on Israel's part." Sounds like a concession, right? Settlements are, in fact, illegal under the Fourth Geneva Convention, to which Israel is a party. Saying they are an immoral blunder is "truthfully deceptive." When you hear Friedman call settlements "a serious moral and strategic error," you don't think, "Oh, he must mean they constitute a violation of international law."

But let me try to find some of Friedman's substantive points to analyze. As he laments the fact that Israel is getting way too much attention, he notes that the Associated Press, his former employer from 2006 to 2011, had over 40 correspondents in Israel during his time there. This number, he notes, was "significantly more news staff than the AP had in China, Russia, or India, or in all of the 50 countries of sub-Saharan Africa combined. It was higher than the total number of news-gathering employees in all the countries where the uprisings of the 'Arab Spring' eventually erupted." I'm not sure why "Arab Spring" was in quotes. It's not a nickname. In any case, Friedman goes to to argue that all these journalists ended up in Israel because Western discourse has "a hostile obsession with Jews."

And there we have it. The media's anti-Israel slant, according to Friedman, is nothing more than institutional anti-Semitism. He never uses the term "anti-Semitism," but he spends a considerable amount of the article saying it over and over. Jews are "the pool into which the world spits." They are "the screen onto which it has become socially acceptable to project the things you hate about yourself and your own country." They are "a symbol of the evils that civilized people are taught from an early age to abhor." The media, writes Friedman, is saying, whether it means to or not, that "Jews are the worst people on earth." He concludes:

Many in the West clearly prefer the old comfort of parsing the moral failings of Jews, and the familiar feeling of superiority this brings them, to confronting an unhappy and confusing reality.

Friedman completely ignores, quite deliberately of course, the possibility that Israel's actions are receiving criticism in the mainstream media because they might actually be immoral, illegal, and indecent. He also leaves out the fact that this phenomenon of media criticism is, in fact, quite new. Finally, he neglects to mention why there is a such a disproportionate number of Western reporters in Israel. They are there precisely because of a decades-long campaign by Israel and its lobbies to tailor the message. They are there at Israel's invitation. They are there because they have been Israel's most effective tool. Until now. Of course, no supporter of Israel was complaining about the huge media presence there when just about every news outlet was towing the party line. But things have changed. And that is what irks Friedman. He is bothered that "truthful deception" is no longer working.

Journalists are starting to ask real questions, and Friedman is not happy about it.

And the questions they are asking are not that crazy:

Why it is ever acceptable to bomb a hospital, school, or UN facility, under any circumstances?

Why does Israel control Gaza's sea, airspace, and entry points, yet continue to tell us there is no military occupation?

Why can a Jewish individual like Matti Friedman, who was born and raised in Canada, automatically receive full citizenship, while millions of Palestinians under Israeli rule in the West Bank and Gaza Strip remain stateless?

I can answer the last question. Israel is a foreign settler enterprise, and foreign settler enterprises need foreign settlers.

Questions like these make people like Matti Friedman very uncomfortable. So, instead of answering them, they simply label those asking them as anti-Semitic. This is the old strategy. And it's not working anymore.

This piece by Friedman played with my emotions a bit, because while it starts out sounding like a possibly interesting take on media coverage of the Gaza War of 2014, it very quickly turns into something I have read a million times before. Friedman's article, while purporting to be some sort of exposé on journalism in Israel, actually turns out to be just another regurgitation of Israel's tired talking points.

Israel is a small country in a sea of hostile Arab nations.
The problem is all these Muslims.
The Palestinians have squandered every opportunity at peace.

Matti, these lines are archaic. You've been using them for 66 years. It's time for them to retire and start collecting Social Security.

On top of calling media criticism of Israel anti-Semitic, Friedman even attempted to label the critics as hypocrites:

White people in London and Paris whose parents not long ago had themselves fanned by dark people in the sitting rooms of Rangoon or Algiers condemn Jewish "colonialism." Americans who live in places called "Manhattan" or "Seat-

tle" condemn Jews for displacing the native people of Palestine. Russian reporters condemn Israel's brutal military tactics. Belgian reporters condemn Israel's treatment of Africans. When Israel opened a transportation service for Palestinian workers in the occupied West Bank a few years ago, American news consumers could read about Israel "segregating buses." And there are a lot of people in Europe, and not just in Germany, who enjoy hearing the Jews accused of genocide.

One should note that Friedman does not deny that Israel is doing any of these things. He is simply saying the critics might be guilty of the same crimes. Well, Mr. Friedman, may I, a lowly Palestinian, who is guilty of none of those terrible things, condemn Israel's colonialism of my native land, displacement of my people, brutal military tactics, ethnic supremacy, and racial segregation? I humbly request your permission.

Ultimately, what scares Matti Friedman more than anything else is why this summer's events in Gaza were, in fact, unique. The discourse is changing. And it is not changing because of anti-Semitism. It is changing because the huge media contingent in Israel, which was for so long reliably echoing its host's case, is now following the lead of us Palestinians and emphatically proclaiming, "The occupier has no clothes!"

The End,

For Now